Making Games

Playful Thinking

Jesper Juul, Geoffrey Long, William Uricchio, and Mia Consalvo, editors

Making Games

The Politics and Poetics of Game Creation Tools

Stefan Werning

The MIT Press
Cambridge, Massachusetts
London, England

This book was set in Stone Serif and Stone Sans by Jen Jackowitz. Printed and bound in the United States of America.

Library of Congress Cataloging-in-Publication Data

Names: Werning, Stefan, author.
Title: Making games : the politics and poetics of game creation tools / Stefan Werning.
Description: Cambridge, Massachusetts : The MIT Press, [2021] | Series: Playful thinking | Includes bibliographical references and index.
Identifiers: LCCN 2020007227 | ISBN 9780262044837 (hardcover)
Subjects: LCSH: Video games--Design. | Video games--Programming. | Video games--Political aspects.
Classification: LCC GV1469.3 .W4787 2021 | DDC 794.8--dc23
LC record available at https://lccn.loc.gov/2020007227

10 9 8 7 6 5 4 3 2 1

Contents

On Thinking Playfully

Many people (we series editors included) find video games exhilarating, but it can be just as interesting to ponder why that is so. What do video games do? What can they be used for? How do they work? How do they relate to the rest of the world? Why is play both so important and so powerful?

Playful Thinking is a series of short, readable, and argumentative books that share some playfulness and excitement with the games that they are about. Each book in the series is small enough to fit in a backpack or coat pocket and combines depth with readability for any reader interested in playing more thoughtfully or thinking more playfully. This includes, but is by no means limited to, academics, game makers, and curious players.

So we are casting our net wide. Each book in our series provides a blend of new insights and interesting arguments with overviews of knowledge from game studies and other areas. You will see this reflected not just in the range of titles in our series, but in the range of authors creating them. Our basic assumption is simple: video games are such a flourishing medium that any new perspective on them is likely to show us something unseen or forgotten, including those from such unconventional voices as artists, philosophers, or specialists in other industries or fields of study. These books are bridge builders, cross-pollinating both areas with new knowledge and new ways of thinking.

At its heart, this is what Playful Thinking is all about: new ways of thinking about games and new ways of using games to think about the rest of the world.

Jesper Juul
Geoffrey Long
William Uricchio
Mia Consalvo

Introduction

The original inspiration for this book comes from years of—usually autodidactic—dabbling in game-making and, later, practice-based game research, starting around 2003 with Macromedia (now Adobe) Flash and the virtually forgotten 3D Game-Studio A5. Macromedia Flash 5 still exhibited numerous traces of its origins as an animation tool, with a strong focus on motion and shape *tweening*—that is, scripted movement and deformation of objects and color gradients, which gave many projects developed with the software a distinct Flash aesthetic. However, trying to make games with Flash 5 was a great entry point into learning to think algorithmically. While practical knowledge of these tools is hardly relevant any longer, the experience itself remains important for me to this day, both professionally and personally.

The tools did not only enable me to make simple games in 2-D and 3-D. As a scholar with a highly eclectic background combining aspects of literary studies, musicology, political sciences, and media, they gave me access to an entirely different epistemology, a way of thinking, in which arguments were not just more or less plausible but some actually *worked* (i.e., were executable and/

or offered a reasonably balanced play experience), while others clearly didn't.

The tools provided a material framework, within which I had to learn to reflect and express myself, quickly becoming part of my identity as an emerging scholar. In her book *Evocative Objects* (2007), Sherry Turkle argues that "we think with the objects we love [and] we love the objects we think with" (5). This claim very distinctly resonated with me as I began to explore other tools, some complex like Unity 3D, others very simple and intuitive to use like Flickgame, which felt even more natural as an extension of my capacity for reflection and self-expression in algorithmic terms. Some objects, which Turkle calls *liminal* with reference to Victor Turner, are evocative because they "are associated with times of transition"—for example, changes in the way we use them over long periods of time, which, in turn, reflect internal changes we may only recognize in retrospect. At this point, I committed to pursuing an academic career, and the ways in which I used game creation software—first as "toys" by myself, later as "tools" for specific purposes together with others— reflected that change in orientation.

Today, there is a plethora of tools that support game creation processes, from prototyping to visual asset creation, authoring, and sound engineering. Many are available for free, featuring accessible interfaces and ready-made sample projects to get started immediately. This includes an increasing number of web applications that do not even require installation, which makes using them feel even more like a technique than a discrete "tool." This inclusiveness frames amateur game-making as an inherently social process, while in the early 2000s it was much more solitary and exclusive. However, even then it was already a distinctly playful process, and every game prototype reflects its author's "playing style." Richard Bartle distinguishes four "archetypes" of players: killers, who play to win over others; achievers, who play to beat the game; explorers, who play to discover new things about the game or themselves; and finally socializers, who play to interact with others. Among these, I clearly identified with the explorer, and most of the prototypes I created reflect that disposition: How can you turn *Asteroids* into a language-learning game? What if Monopoly were a one-player game? Would the *Grand Theft Auto* series work as a board game? If so, how? I usually considered questions like these more interesting to "explore" using game creation tools than learning how to make the "best" first-person shooter—which Bartle would associate with the achiever's approach—or joining other people's game jam projects as a socializer, that is, primarily for the sake of social interaction. These approaches are certainly just as relevant but indicative of different playing styles. At Utrecht University, I continue to explore how game-making can transcend the creative industries and gradually become a cultural and communicative practice like writing or photography, as well as how new tools promise to push that practice in exciting new directions.

1 Making Sense of Tools

#IDARB and the Many Sides of Game Tools

In early January 2014, game developer Mike Mika set out to create a game in his spare time, potentially together with some friends. Mika had been developing games since the 1980s and, at the time, was working at Other Ocean, a company mainly creating licensed games, as well as a few of their own design, such as the *Puffins* series (2010) and *The War of the Worlds* (2011). Because his job as a professional game developer did not allow him to share what he was working on, Mika wanted his own development experience to be more social—similar to how games were created in the 1980s and early 1990s in smaller teams. He took to Twitter, posting a picture of his first prototype and the following message: "Where to go with this? I've started a new project, it draws a red box. Thinking platformer. #helpmedev."[1] As with many Twitter conversations, the first reactions were humorous, sometimes witty but rather tangential. For instance, game developer Tim Schafer wrote in response: "I think the red box needs to make a critical choice, and the narrative branches from there." However, this seemingly erratic back-and-forth sparked interest in the game until the Twitter comments became more focused, starting with Bob Koon's suggestion that the red box could "hang/walk on the ceilings" and might receive "health penalties for standing/walking."[2] From there, the process gained more and more momentum, and, according to *WIRED*, the tweet "turned into the best new multiplayer game in years," later titled *#IDARB* (2015) and backed by Microsoft's ID@Xbox initiative.[3]

#IDARB is a peculiar case even within the broad and often colorful field of independent games. Its creation is technically a form of software development, but the unique process and the combination of tools and practices involved can, for instance, be more productively compared to improvisational theater.[4] Game design scholars have already tentatively explored theatrical improvisation as a potential role model for game design (O'Shaughnessy and Ward 2014). However, this model was specifically applied to the design of a "multiplayer physical game" (588) that uses digital technology but foregrounds real-world social interaction. Instead, theater as a metaphor to understand the unique relationship that Mike Mika developed with his "audience" and the way in which the "spectators" became co-creators is more broadly applicable and emphasizes the fact that rather than simply leading up to the final product, the process is meaningful in and of itself. Despite its uniqueness, though, *#IDARB* exemplifies several important characteristics of contemporary digital games.

First, it points to the inherent tension between cultures of independent game production built on informal networking (Guevara-Villalobos 2011, 6) and sharing (7), and the logic of the commercial game industry. Collaborating with Microsoft increased the game's outreach but became a point of contention with the *#IDARB* audience.

Second, on a related note, the project demonstrates that user participation is not simply a quantity that can and should be increased (Brandt 2006) but can refer to a broad spectrum of potential involvement. Many games provide in-game tools that incentivize but also streamline user-created content, but *#IDARB* defined its own rules of play for community activity on Twitter but otherwise did not intervene very much. For instance, the game *Please be nice :(* (2014), developed by Aran Koning at around the same time as *#IDARB*, demonstrates yet another form of community engagement by allowing the first player to successfully complete the respective latest version of the game to suggest one new feature to be implemented in the next iteration.[5]

Third, *#IDARB* emphasized the fact that the distribution of a computer game produces a distinct, increasingly curated choreography and becomes part of the game experience, blurring the boundary between making and playing.[6] For instance, Mike Mika implemented so-called hashbombs—that is, specific words or phrases sent via Twitter or Twitch that trigger a predefined event in a currently active game session, such as flooding the arena or turning all players into *Minecraft* characters. Because the feature was known but the code words were secret, players tried every word they could think of to see if they could affect the gameplay, thereby producing waves of cascading social media activity that dramatically increased the game's outreach. Although this metagame element had no explicitly specified rules, it worked by affording distinct patterns of play. Every successfully guessed term would refine the collective mental model—the group's understanding which types of key words might likely be selected as hashbombs—and thus its capacity to play efficiently. Moreover, it rekindled player engagement by demonstrating that this game could be won and thereby produced a specific rhythm or choreography.

Fourth, *#IDARB* clearly reflects the gradual personalization of (independent) game-making. Formerly, Mike Mika was a little-known designer and programmer, but he became the players' window into the game, shaping their interpretation of and personal identification with its design. Mika is active on both Twitter and Vine, and the combination of these brief verbal and visual impressions was interpreted by players as part of a coherent narrative.[7] For example, in one popular video, the programmer demonstrates a version of the arcade game *Donkey Kong*, which he hacked for his daughter to enable her to play as Pauline rescuing Jumpman.[8] Several years earlier, he had made news by hiding his marriage proposal in the puzzle game *Klax*, which he ported to the Game Boy Color at the time.[9] These emotionally relatable micronarratives were interpreted as part of an archetypal story, which—as implied in the comparison with improvisational theater—made the creation of games like *#IDARB* "performative" (Kattenbelt 2010). That is, the game does not simply come to exist but is the result of a performance, an act of staging by an individual who engages in a reciprocal relationship with an audience. Similarly, social media activities such as Twitter discussions on currently airing episodes can turn television production into a "'live' performance" (Thompson 2012). While the production and reception of prerecorded television episodes are usually not synchronized, introducing a newly cast character or unveiling a much-anticipated plot twist becomes more personal because producers and viewers are simultaneously active on the same social media platform, aware of each other's presence.

Finally, and most importantly, *#IDARB* demonstrates the relevance of tools as an important but still often overlooked aspect of digital games and the creative industries in general. For instance, the cultivation of a recognizable creator personality like Mike Mika is facilitated or even required by crowdfunding tools like Kickstarter. Crowdfunding has become more and more important for both up-and-coming developers and industry veterans. Industry celebrities like Tim Schafer, Chris Roberts, and Richard Garriott have successfully told their own origin stories to pitch new projects. But lesser-known game designers also need to define a memorable story about why or how they want to create their game.[10] Kickstarter's defining features, such as the central pitch video and the multitude of similar, concurrently crowdfunded projects on the same platform, require developers to address their intended audience personally and control their own narrative to stand out.[11]

The game #IDARB itself was developed using a proprietary game engine that Other Ocean had used for its previous project.[12] However, its design was profoundly shaped by the use of Twitter and its characteristic features, such as retweets, image sharing, and the overall focus on real-time, short-form communication. Thus, game development requires the interplay of many tools and users, and in this constellation, Twitter can be just as relevant as a proper game engine like Unity, just fulfilling a different purpose. One way to understand the relevance of Twitter in the context of #IDARB is as a platform designed to grow, structure, and maintain an active user community (around the game).[13] Dutch media scholars Sabine Niederer and José van Dijk define this as a *sociotechnical system*. For instance, in the case of Wikipedia (Niederer and van Dijck 2010), the reputation system (1372) is vital for structuring the community, increasing the users' identification with and sense of place within the constantly growing user group. Moreover, the bots used for routine tasks on Wikipedia ensure constant frictionless interaction within the community (1377)—for instance, by creating placeholder entries that encourage human editors to fill in the gaps. Similarly, the use of Twitter and the frequent *#IDARB* prototypes created a shared sense of progress among the community, playtesting prevented the design from falling apart, and the backlog of messages on Twitter provided an entry point into the community and its shared history for potential new members.

The impact that its development history had on *#IDARB* as a product is difficult to measure; launching as a temporary Microsoft exclusive and a comparatively high price point limited its mainstream market appeal, but user reviews indicate the uncommonly intense dedication of its fans.[14] Unpacking the implications of *#IDARB* has been a first step toward developing a critical vocabulary for the analysis of tool design, similar to the numerous conceptual frameworks that exist for the study of games themselves.[15] The next step will be to outline a working definition of (game creation) tools, which allows for situating them within a broader cultural context of tool-making and tool use.

Toward an Extended Definition of Tools

The goal of this book is to make sense of the increasing abundance of game-making tools and to conceptualize their influence on both the politics and aesthetics of digital games. In existing cultural analyses of game production (Martin and Deuze 2009; O'Donnell 2014; Vanderhoef and Curtin 2016), tools play a minor role. For instance, in her analysis of game design processes at Valve Corporation and Linden Lab, van der Graaf (2012) primarily examines the organizational forms both companies adopted to structure their design work and the roles of individual employees within these structures.[16] With its focus on the diverse functions of tools, the book at hand contributes to these existing studies of game production. However, by situating its case studies within broader cultural and historical contexts of tool-making and tool use, it aims to provide a conceptual framework that can also be adapted to different media industries, such as development tools for mobile applications or YouTube content.[17] For that purpose, the book operates with a more expansive definition of tools than those often used in common or industry parlance (e.g., game development website Gamasutra's Tool Postmortem series), which usually refer to software programs used for the creation of game content.[18] Although additional defining criteria will be discussed throughout the book, this definition relies on four basic characteristics:

(1) *Tool use occurs all across the value chain (or value network, rather than just in the creation of game content* (see, e.g., Stabell and Fjeldstad 1998). That is, contrary to the previously indicated focus on production, this also includes the use of Gantt charts during the planning phase or of an Excel or Google spreadsheet to manage the delivery of merchandise to Kickstarter backers. Moreover, game creation tools bridge the epistemic gap between tools for amateur users (e.g., Scratch, RPG Maker), ambitious laymen (e.g., GameMaker: Studio, Construct 2), semiprofessionals (e.g., Unity), and industry professionals (e.g., Unreal Engine, CryEngine). This situation offers ample opportunities to observe how these tools shape the cultural imaginary of games as a medium in transition.

(2) *Tools are manipulatable and shareable objects.* This might seem commonsensical, but two examples from the history of art production provided by American sociologist Howard S. Becker demonstrate the relevance of this characteristic. For instance, Becker points out how Victorian novelist Anthony Trollope would get up early enough in the morning to "get in his three

hours of writing before going to work as a civil servant in the British Post Office" (Becker 1982, 19); as this practice likely had a noticeable impact on Trollope's writing, it might count as a *technique*—a denotation that I will explore further—but not as a tool. On the contrary, contracts between fifteenth-century clients and painters, specifying, for example, the use of materials such as "powdered gold" and "ultramarine of the value about four florins the ounce" (15), have a material form; that is, they are (at least potentially) manipulatable and shareable.

This material quality affords several important forms of tool use such as customization. Books like Eric Sloane's *A Museum of Early American Tools* from 1964 illustrate that making tools (and making them one's own) has been an important aspect of performing not only the craftsman's professional and personal identity but even their cultural identity. The idea of a craftsman customizing their tools to fit (and thus reflect) their own work habits also applies to UI layout modification and plug-in selection in digital tools such as Eclipse (Draxler et al. 2012).

(3) *Tools shape the relationships between different stakeholders.* As indicated by the previous example of contracts used to commission artworks, tools are objects that can be accessed and manipulated by multiple stakeholders and, therefore, regulate interactions and relationships between them. A common example from media production is the *story bible* (Parkin 2009, 15), a document used by many TV drama series to maintain narrative coherence by explicating character profiles and available sets; all departments need to abide by it. Thus, while a story bible—similar to a game design document—does not create content, it essentially organizes the collaboration between different production domains, thereby indirectly shaping the final product.[19] American sociologist Susan Leigh Star uses the term *boundary*

objects to describe this structuring function of material objects (Leigh Star 2010). The author specifically refers to both physical and digital objects in various professional contexts such as maps or diagrams that, by way of their interpretive flexibility, afford different interpretations by different groups but also, through their immutable aspects, create a common ground for reaching a shared understanding between those groups. Boell and Hoof (2015) illustrate this with reference to the role Gantt charts play in corporate organizations: while each department reads these documents slightly differently, their unchanging object properties allow for observing these differences and indirectly regulating the relationships and interactions between these groups. Based on this defining characteristic, content produced using digital development tools—for example, interactive prototypes using placeholder art—can itself become a tool that regulates the boundary between different stakeholders, such as programmers and artists or the development team and potential publishing partners.[20]

Jennifer Whitson applies the notion of game creation tools as boundary objects to emphasize how complex tools like Unity are considered "magical" (2322) or even "agential" (2328), having a life of their own because they exhibit "recalcitrant, willful" (2322)—that is, unpredictable—behavior. Whitson demonstrates how the concept can be useful for an ethnographic approach, pointing to the term *voodoo software* (2324) that developers attribute to these tools, which implicitly connotes their relationship with the tool and the priest-like role they define for themselves as its users.[21] This book aims to provide a complementary focus on how the design of tools affects their function as boundary objects.

(4) *Tools meaningfully frame the purpose they are intended for.* As suggested by the famous dictum (often attributed to eminent

psychologist Abraham Maslow) that "if the only tool you have is a hammer, [you] treat everything as if it were a nail" (Gardien et al. 2014), over-relying on one familiar tool is both very common and problematic. Yet beyond the warning implied in this *law of the instrument* (as philosopher Abraham Kaplan called it in 1964), the claim more neutrally implies that tools characteristically shape our understanding of the material they process and therefore our understanding of the problem at hand. For instance, while pitching *Super Mario Maker* at its 2015 E3 press conference, Nintendo unveiled the graph paper sheets that were used to plan the levels for the original *Super Mario Bros.* on the NES.[22]

These sheets not only were handed to the programmers to be translated into code, but—through constant use—also became a cognitive filter, which shaped the development team's

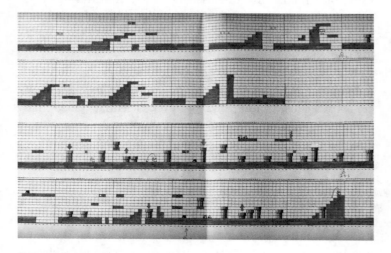

Figure 1.1
Graph paper used in the design of Super Mario Bros.; screenshot taken from https://youtu.be/DLoRd6_a1CI at 2'56".

perception of the content (e.g., by affording a view of the visual composition of the whole level at a glance) and their imaginary of possible *Super Mario Bros.* levels. Similarly, switching from assembler code to C++ in the creation of *Sonic Spinball* (1993) reflected a trade-off Sega management was willing to make: using C++ resulted in the game running at a lower framerate but enabled the developers to complete it in time before the holiday season.[23]

Following that definition, games themselves increasingly become tools for other purposes. For instance, online video creators use games (and the franchises behind them) as tools to carve out a niche for themselves within the YouTube ecosystem via Let's Play or Unboxing videos. At the same time, as implied by analyses of Let's Play videos (Burwell and Miller 2016), the videos themselves can be understood as tools to develop game literacy and as boundary objects that frame the relationships between producers and consumers in the digital game industry. Furthermore, many players use online games as de facto social networks, as tools to cope with stressful experiences, or, through modding tools, as a medium for expressing their personality and opinions (Werning 2018b).[24]

This book combines two important dimensions of game creation tools—politics and poetics—to situate them more broadly within cultural traditions of tool-making and tool-use. Popular franchises and hardware platforms maybe have a more evident impact on the *political economy* of the (digital) game industry, but even though the role tools play in this context might be subtler, it is just as important. Media practitioners and scholars like Bertolt Brecht and Hans-Magnus Enzensberger had already acknowledged the importance of access to and knowledge of media-making tools early in the twentieth century, urging contemporary societies to "place the means of media production 'in the hands of the masses themselves'" (qtd. in Jenkins 2014). Tools thus essentially shape what media scholar Henry Jenkins calls the "terms of our participation" (273) in media culture, by which he refers to fan engagement with media franchises but also simultaneously to broader "political participation" (285). This requires a debate about "values [that] emerge from the tools that we build and how we choose to use them" (Friedman 1996), which especially took hold as computer-based tools became more pervasive and differentiated during the 1990s.

In the current media environment, many major companies produce and distribute tools, many of which are not even directly related to their core business. For instance, Disney has been making its proprietary tools accessible via an open-source program.[25] This includes both software like Ptex, which is used by Walt Disney Animation Studios to create 3-D content, and tool collections performing more mundane internal tasks, like Munki, which enables administrators to manage software installs. For Disney, this move is part of a larger strategy to attract the most capable talents. From the users' perspective, on the other hand, it removes an imagined barrier between their lived experience and "the industry"—like how, until recently, amateur filmmakers had not been able to use the same (prohibitively expensive) cameras as industry professionals.[26] That is, it enables ambitious hobbyists to "role-play" being (or becoming) part of the creative industries. This newfound emphasis on tool strategies also goes beyond traditional media companies. For instance, in 2017, ridesharing service Uber released Pyro, a probabilistic programming language. Uber's long-term vision relies on constant growth, which requires a combination of data science and artificial intelligence to find optimal routes, ride-pooling opportunities, and the like to scale their business activities. According to Uber AI Labs, the team behind Pyro, the company has shared the tool "to encourage the scientific world to collaborate on making AI tools more flexible, open, and easy-to-use."[27] A year earlier, Amazon had launched a proprietary game engine, Lumberyard, as part of its multistage strategy to evolve into a media creation platform, using game-making as a catalyst to propagate its core businesses such as Amazon Web Services (AWS) and the recently acquired streaming service Twitch. Thus, game creation tools are of particular political-economic relevance—in the sense that they enable companies to adopt platform strategies and gain a broader foothold in the digital economy—because they are increasingly used also for the creation of interactive media content other than entertainment games. For instance, the popular game engine Unity is also commonly used to create apps and nongame software.[28]

Although their economic relevance appears intuitively plausible, the impact that tools have on the aesthetics strategies of (digital) games requires more explanation. This view on the interplay of distinct design elements is usually referred to as *poetics* (for an application of Aristotle's original concept to contemporary televisual narratives, see, e.g., Newman 2006). While the case studies throughout this book will elaborate on how tools meaningfully constrain and inform the composition of digital games, the example of asset marketplaces such as the Unity Asset Store might serve as an entry point into this discussion.[29] In the early 1990s, anyone wanting to create a *Star Wars* fan game would have had to create all audiovisual assets from scratch, including a font that resembles the movie's logo and promotional texts, 3-D models of the iconic spaceships, and sound effects.[30] This top-down approach to appropriating a franchise like *Star Wars* is characterized by a specific rationality, such as having to think about specific colors, dimensions, and proportions, as well as potentially sampling voice snippets from the original movie trilogy.[31] In contrast, today all audiovisual assets are already easily and usually freely available, often in multiple versions on asset marketplaces like 3D Warehouse.[32]

These tools afford different ways of conceptualizing fan games based on the *Star Wars* franchise. Most importantly, rather than having to create content, amateur creators primarily select from a vast, freely sortable array of preexisting content. New media scholar Lev Manovich calls this the "logic of selection" (Manovich 2001, 123), arguing that selection becomes a productive practice in and of itself. Writing in 1999, Manovich noticed that contemporary software tools increasingly provided

Figure 1.2
Screenshot of Star Wars–themed content at 3D Warehouse, the online platform for Google's 3D modeling software SketchUp

ready-made content, such as "textures and icons supplied by paint programs [and] 3-D models that come with a 3-D modeling program" (127); compared with the current situation, opportunities for applying the logic of selection have multiplied. The default view after searching for "Star Wars" on 3D Warehouse visually juxtaposes very different types of content, including many variations of Star Destroyers, the iconic capital ships, but also a 3-D model of the franchise logo, several *Star Wars* LEGO models, and even the *Star Wars*–themed All Nippon Airways Boeing jets that promoted the launch of the third movie trilogy in 2016. Seeing all these ready-mades in parallel inherently guides but also constrains the designer's imagination and, thus, the spectrum of potential game designs. This approach towards intellectual work and innovation has been referred to as *bricolage*, a term by which Claude Levi-Strauss originally defined a form of craftsmanship using "only the tools and materials 'at-hand'" (Rogers 2012, 1). Applied to fan game creation as in the case discussed here, it describes an "[emergent] construction . . . that changes and takes new forms as the bricoleur adds different tools, methods, and techniques of representation and interpretation to the puzzle" (5)—that is, a bottom-up approach characteristically different from commercial game production. For instance, while most of the top-ranked *Star Wars* models (sorted by relevance) in the 3D Warehouse collection represent spaceships, the location that seems to have most thoroughly captured the modelers' imagination is the city-planet Coruscant. Thus, for reasons of feasibility, bricoleur developers may use these models "at hand" as a starting point from which they derive game mechanics and narratives in an emergent design process.

Finally, asset marketplaces afford comparing the most popular types of content and the most positively rated designs within the community—not least because, by default, available assets are sorted by relevance. Thus, with each search operation, users inherently develop and incrementally refine an intuitive understanding of how other creators interpret the franchise, including but not limited to the disproportionate iconicity of Star Destroyers. Thus, numerous asynchronous interactions with the tool gradually produce a sense of "imagined community" among its users, similar to interactions among Twitter users (see Gruzd, Wellman, and Takhteyev 2011), who also do not communicate directly but develop a shared sense of group identity.

Now that we have established a working definition that combines political and aesthetic aspects of tools, it is time to investigate more specific game creation contexts. Understanding them as sociotechnical systems as suggested earlier is one potentially fruitful way to conceptualize that role, but there are more. Ahead, several other theoretical lenses—thinking of the definition of *lenses* that Schell (2014) uses to study game design—will be introduced, which, taken together, outline a production studies perspective on digital game creation.

A Production Studies Perspective on Digital Game Creation

As of March 2017, the Game Creation Tools Classification archive lists more than 491 entries, ranging from general-purpose game engines to highly focused programs such as Arcade Game Studio, dedicated to producing very specific types of games.[33] This diversity seems counterintuitive because in commercial game design only a handful of tools, such as the Unreal Engine or the Unity engine, prove competitive enough to become de facto industry standards. Thus, it appears that all these tools fulfill purposes other than simply getting the job done, and understanding these purposes requires looking at digital games from a production studies standpoint.

So far, media scholars have mostly investigated production contexts with regard to film (Mayer, Banks, and Caldwell 2009) and television (Caldwell 2004). For instance, the gradual shift from documentary to fictional forms in early film between 1903 and 1904 marked a profound change for film as a medium (Heidenreich 2004). However, this change was driven primarily by the inability of production companies to continually find relevant real-world events to cover (162) rather than the creative impetus of contemporary directors. Moreover, chase scenes (163) presented a notable logistical challenge due to the frequent change of locations, which production teams "solved" by beginning to shoot scenes by location (rather than according to script chronology) and by developing new tools such as smaller and more lightweight cameras. These investments, in turn, "required" companies to implement chase scenes at scale, thereby fostering their formal diversity and, ultimately, their elevation to a versatile aesthetic device in films like *The General* (1927) and *Stagecoach* (1939).[34]

By way of a historical comparison, the relevance of production tools and techniques can also be observed in less commercial domains such as art (Becker 1982). The production process of both art and games has been characteristically mystified in public discourses, albeit for slightly different reasons. To lift that veil, Becker points out, for instance, how artists standardize their daily routines and how they stay productive by rationalizing their own processes. Moreover, as indicated in the introduction, the commissioning of an artwork was specified in highly detailed contracts, which would even determine the physical composition of colors or which parts of an artwork could be delegated to subcontractors (15). While these mundane specifications are incompatible with popular discourses on art, they tangibly affected its creation, such as by acting as material constraints. Much like arbitrary constraints in a game challenge players to improvise within well-defined boundaries (Suits 1967), innovative artists used these constraints to unlock their creativity in a playful manner. This playful use of tools also applies to game-making tools, mostly in the context of independent game development but also, as demonstrated in the case studies ahead, in larger game studios. For instance, game jams constitute playful competitions, playgrounds in which aspiring developers can demonstrate—among other qualities—the mastery of their tools. Notch, the original creator of the immensely popular sandbox game *Minecraft*, honed his Java skills by participating in the Ludum Dare game jam from 2008 on before putting these skills to use in his magnum opus.[35] Moreover, the game jams arguably served as palate cleansers, sharpening his design sensibilities between more commercially oriented projects. As we will elaborate ahead, other game-specific concepts such as cheating can be similarly used as lenses to obtain a different view of contemporary game-making. Based on extensive interviews with players, Mia Consalvo defines *cheating* as a transgressive practice, toward both other players and the game itself (Consalvo 2007), but her examples also indicate that it constitutes a particular way of learning about games, of building up game literacy. Similarly, game creators try to push the boundaries of their tools and try to find uses for them that the developers might have never anticipated: for instance, a programmer going by the name crruzi on Reddit turned Microsoft Excel into a game-making tool and used it to recreate the iconic strategy game mechanics of the *XCOM* franchise.[36] Similar to a player resorting to cheating in a game, crruzi attempted to maximize his performance in Visual Basic for Applications, the scripting language behind the Microsoft Office tools, and in the process learned about the mechanics of Excel by systematically testing its boundaries.

Unlike earlier production analyses of film and TV, production analyses of digital games (O'Donnell 2014; van der Graaf 2012) usually do not establish a clear connection between socioeconomic contexts (which include development tools) and their effects on the design of the games themselves. In one of the most recent handbooks on production studies, a dedicated section promises a critical investigation of "tools of the trade" (Banks, Conor, and Mayer 2016, 1–36). Yet the three papers cover chat bots, stardom, and labor division in prop making and thus do not attempt to provide a systematic, comparative understanding of tools. To address this, the remainder of this chapter outlines six critical perspectives on tools in digital game production, which will serve as a conceptual framework for the case studies in chapter 2.

Tools and the Ontologies of Digital Games

Most basically, each tool characteristically frames and institutionalizes the user's perception of the media content it processes. That is, depending on the things they allow (and don't allow) users to do with a material (e.g. a 3-D model in Autodesk Maya or a texture in Photoshop), tools encourage users to focus on specific aspects over others and to envision specific ways of using a material.

This does not exclusively apply to digital media; for example, the technical development of musical instruments has profoundly shaped contemporary views of musical aesthetics.[37] However, the even more rapid changes that software tools undergo affect the ontology of digital images and videos to an unprecedented degree.[38] Media scholar and designer Lev Manovich has addressed these changes in his seminal book *The Language of New Media* (2001) and even more systematically in his analyses of Adobe After Effects (Manovich 2007) and Adobe Photoshop (Manovich 2011). In the process, he identifies distinct interface elements such as the organization of digital video clips in a timeline view or the concept of digital image layers, which can be algorithmically blended. According to this view, After Effects has been instrumental in promoting the visual hybridity and remixing of visual traditions characteristic of digital media culture—for instance, by combining elements of photography, video typography, and interactivity.

Borrowing terminology from actor-network theory (Latour 2007), which has been a popular frame of reference in media production analyses (see, e.g., Teurlings 2013 on television production), Manovich attributes a lot of agency to one specific tool. Actor-network theory characteristically does not distinguish between human and nonhuman agents—for example, between users and software tools—and regards both as parts of networks that form a "system of alliances" (Sismondo 2011, 82). Thus, while users make use of technologies, they are themselves also used by technologies to support the unique interests built into them (Miettinen 1999, 181). Accordingly, After Effects itself can be regarded as a nonhuman actor or, more precisely, as an actor-network—that is, as a set consisting of technological features but also, for instance, sample assets provided with the software (which, especially with less experienced users, shape the visual imagination) and less tangible "actors," such as stratified user expectations from previous experience with related tools.

Similarly, Microsoft PowerPoint frames how users think about a given subject matter—that is, how they plan an argument as a sequence of virtual slides with imagined transitions. The fact that these slides are organized in time rather than space (such as in the competing software Prezi, which offers an infinite canvas for users to arrange their slides within) is part of what German media historians Claus Pias and Wolfgang Coy describe as a *distinct ideology* (Pias 2009) embedded into the software technology. Through repeated use, this ideology can even influence entire schools of thought. For instance, art historians have traditionally used diapositives and, later, sequences of images in extensive, mostly uncommented PowerPoint presentations in their research practice.[39] Beat Wyss argues that this material practice contributed to framing art history as a primarily philological (rather than systematic) discipline (Wyss 2009), a form of scholarship that focuses on identifying aesthetic continuities rather than, for instance, constructing models of artistic activity and works.

Similarly, tools for writing games institutionalize consensual perceptions of digital games that cannot be observed just by playing a game, similar to how viewing a digital image on a screen does not reveal the underlying layers. However, by modding (Sotamaa 2010) or (re)making games themselves, players learn to look behind the scenes and intuitively include this in their shared knowledge of the medium. For instance, instead of the layers in Photoshop, Unity offers a modular inspector view of in-game objects, in which behavior scripts, as well as rendering properties, collision boxes, and sound emitters, appear as conceptual "layers" that can even be independently activated and deactivated just like image layers. Unlike the timeline view of After Effects, Unity cannot visualize the systemic behavior of the game over time, but it characteristically enables an almost real-time switching between play mode and develop mode, which allows the developer to make rapid parameter changes and quickly compare the results. Even closer to After Effects, the Unreal Engine pioneered visual programming interfaces (labeled Kismet in Unreal Engine 3 and Blueprint in Unreal Engine 4) as a key visual metaphor, which indicates the flow of information among in-game objects and thus structures the developer's mental model of the game.

Finally, Unity and most other 3-D game engines use a comparatively large, interactive previsualization window into the virtual environment as their central UI element. Users can partly customize what will be displayed in this scene view, which represents sounds, cameras, and light sources as wireframe icons, but the graphical quality is reminiscent of the final game, and

Figure 1.3
IMG-ue4blueprint. Blueprint in an official Unreal Engine video tutorial (https://www.youtube.com/watch?v=gHdwOiR0D0A).

the camera position can be freely moved, rotated, and zoomed.[40] This visual dispositif is characteristically similar to that used in the making of 3-D blockbuster movies, pioneered by James Cameron and the virtual camera technology developed for *Avatar* (2009).[41]

This technology allows the director to move and look around a green screen set while seeing the previsualized scene in real time through a virtual ocular. As with Unity, it institutionalized the precedence of topography presented primarily in perspective projection. At the same time, however, it encourages directors/designers to focus on framing and mise-en-scène while approaching new scenes and to use the simulated space as a way of "solving" narrative "problems."[42] For the film *The Jungle Book* (2016), a more advanced previsualization tool called Photon was

Figure 1.4
The virtual camera setup used during the filming of Avatar (https://www.wired.com/2009/11/ff_avatar_5steps/).

used, and it enabled the cinematographer not only to plan the composition of the scene but also to "direct lights, pull focus on the lens, add dynamic atmospheric effects such as rain, fog, fire, and essentially dictate the mood of a shot."[43]

Over time, the focus of these activities has shifted to commercial off-the-shelf (COTS) software, and plug-ins have turned Unity into an established previsualization solution for film and television productions (see, e.g., De Goussencourt and Bertolino 2015). For instance, the popular Cinema Pro Cams toolkit simulates different types of lenses and allegedly affords "learning the ins-and-outs of camera behavior and technology, camera settings and how those settings affect the final image."[44] By referencing established brands (e.g., ARRI or SIRT) and concepts (e.g., f-stop settings and industry standard aspect ratio selection), these applications aim to blur the epistemic boundary between analogue film production and genuinely digital design practices such as computer and console (because, e.g., board game development cannot be considered "genuinely digital") game development.

Tools as Platforms

Previously, I proposed to understand tools as highly fragile constellations of algorithms, mechanics built into user interfaces, and conventions that keep a user community sustainable, productive, and allow it to scale—that is, sociotechnical systems (Niederer and van Dijck 2010). To fulfill that purpose, tools need to constantly change and expand, enabling their developers to forge strategic alliances; in that sense, they need to be regarded as platforms (Bogost and Montfort 2007).

Accordingly, platforms are "whatever the programmer takes for granted when developing, and whatever . . . the user is required to have working to use particular software." They are programmable systems that sit below four other layers of abstraction: code, form/function, interface, and finally reception/operation—that is, the users themselves (Bogost and Montfort 2007, 177–178).

A different definition by American entrepreneur and investor Marc Andreessen instead emphasizes the fact that the programmability of a platform and the gaps in its existing functionality structure the ecosystem of developers flocking around it: "A 'platform' is a system that can be programmed and therefore customized by outside developers—users—and in that way, adapted to countless needs and niches that the platform's original developers could not have possibly contemplated, much less had time to accommodate."[45]

The platform definition characteristically also applies to games-as-tools like *ARK: Survival Evolved* (2015), which users have repeatedly tailored to their own needs and which have over time spawned their own modding subcultures and organized communities.[46] This increasingly common category of (mostly) digital games epitomizes the principle of user-driven innovation, achieved by "repartitioning development tasks" into "toolkits" (Von Hippel 2001, 250), which Eric von Hippel has been advocating since the early 2000s. Von Hippel addresses product customization and personalization in different industries, including food design (250), cars (251), and even hairstyling (252), arguing that customer needs and wants are becoming too granular and fleeting for companies to respond to. In comparison, games are rather unique products, but in all these cases, conceptualizing a product as platform goes beyond maximizing convenience and usability to acknowledge the act of customization itself as a form of self-expression.

Similar to hardware platforms such as the Atari VCS (Bogost and Montfort 2007, 178) and the Nintendo Wii (186), game engines are also programmable and serve as "material constraint[s]" (176). For instance, from the perspective of developers only using Unity, the game engine black-boxes the actual constraints of the hardware and replaces them with its own. Unlike hardware specifications, which evolve more slowly and are reflected by high-level graphics APIs such as DirectX and OpenGL, Unity characteristically loosens its own constraints and introduces new affordances at regular, more frequent intervals with every new software update.[47] Here, Lev Manovich's focus on the most popular, monolithic software packages still appears intuitively plausible because the market for game engines is highly oligopolistic, with Unreal Engine 4 and Unity (among others) in key positions. However, a more comprehensive analysis of media tools needs to pursue a closer look and a more thoroughly comparative perspective. As argued earlier, multitudes of smaller, more idiosyncratic tools exist within these large software ecosystems (Jansen, Finkelstein, and Brinkkemper 2009) or, increasingly, form their own, more specialized and fleeting ecosystems. Finally, game tools also become part of ecosystems that extend further than the digital games economy per se. For instance, Amazon recently released Lumberyard, a free and open-source game engine that characteristically integrates with Amazon Web Services and with Twitch, a streaming platform for game-related content acquired by Amazon in 2014.[48] Thus, the tool can and should be regarded as a cornerstone in the company's attempt to consolidate its status as a platform among the likes of Google and Facebook rather than "mere" game companies like Unity Technologies (Unity) and Epic Games (Unreal Engine).

While the platform qualities of tools will be further expounded in the case studies ahead, it is important to acknowledge that the *platform*, a term usually reserved for online social networks like Facebook and Twitter, is first and foremost a metaphor. As such, it may make very different phenomena called platforms appear more comparable than they really are. It also effectively conceals the fact that they are not uniform but "intricate and multilayered landscapes, . . . populated by many, diverse, sometimes overlapping, and sometimes contentious communities" (Gillespie 2017). The dynamics within these communities will be the focus of the following section.

Tool Communities

Programmability also is a key aspect of the formation and differentiation of *tool communities*—that is, more or less formalized groups of individuals and small studios that emerge around popular software applications. For example, one key feature in earlier versions of Unity was the coexistence of JavaScript (or, rather, a syntactically related but Unity-specific scripting language) and C#, both of which could be used within the same project.[49] The former was primarily addressed at hobbyists, while the latter was aimed more at professionals. Users would find code examples in both languages online and could mix and match them in their projects. This interchangeability allowed Unity to become a point of transition between these formerly divided groups, thereby diversifying its community. Amateurs potentially become more engaged by the prospect of finding their way into the industry, while professional developers can build their own followings by sharing knowledge, thereby promoting their studios (e.g., in preparation for a crowdfunding campaign). Both groups, albeit in different ways, consider game-making an important part of their identity and become invested in their tool of choice, not unlike how fans become invested in media franchises (Jenkins 2006, 27, 57). They develop an emotional connection based on accumulating positive (and, to a lesser degree, negative) experiences over time and are compelled to defend them against proponents of other tools/franchises.

To further investigate this aspect, it is imperative to consider how tools change and (re)position themselves over time to create and sustain communities. A prominent recent example is the rivalry between Adobe Flash (Salter and Murray 2014) and HTML5, a conflict between two interactive web (and, not least, game) technologies that was notably framed by external platforms like iOS.[50] This conflict will be revisited in chapter 2 in the section on tool fandom, because it was played out across the two rivaling tool communities. Many people had previously built a living on becoming expert users of Flash and now had to reposition themselves, either by switching to HTML5 or, as many did, by siding with Flash and trying to create content that would demonstrate the assumed superiority of the platform and would make it harder for Apple to ignore it. More recently, the gradual shift of game development tools from products to services has had a tangible effect on the affective relationship between users and their tools.[51] Although monthly subscription payments are primarily intended to hamper software piracy, they also foster a heightened sense of loyalty by requiring customers to "perform" their affiliation through a continuous (and thus more tangible) investment, rather than a one-time payment. Sections in chapter 2 that focus on creator identities and tool fandom respectively will provide further evidence of social tool use and demonstrate how tool use can be instrumental in shaping and performing group membership.

Tools between Artifacts and Practices

As argued in the introduction, the notion of tools primarily refers to a self-contained artifact (i.e., a physical or digital object), but with repeated use or by more or less seamlessly combining different tools into a workflow, this object quality can become all but invisible to the tool user. Therefore, it is important to also consider networks of associated tools (that is, in actor-network theory terminology, *alliances* shaped through technical integration and through simply symbiotic use; see, e.g., Sismondo 2011, 82) that enable both intended and unintended usage practices.

The example of *#IDARB* demonstrated the blurring of boundaries between tools as actual software programs, web-based platforms like Twitter, and improvised, partially formalized means of altering the production process that are part technique (Agazzi 1998) and part technology. For instance, Mike Mika used a Google spreadsheet to compile Twitter responses, rating them by feasibility and humor.[52] This might seem like a curiously idiosyncratic but ultimately irrelevant practice, but our means of writing and storing information has profound implications for the way we think. This includes many factors, such as the weight of the pen, the dimensions of the sheet of paper, our own body posture while writing, and, for digital technologies, the functionalities of software like Microsoft Word or, in this case, Google Docs. Media historian Jay Bolter summarizes this influence by arguing that the materiality of writing technologies—that is, the "writing space" (Bolter 2001)—frames our "economies of writing" (21) and thus compels us to think and speak according to literary conventions and habits. Again, this is not limited to literary techniques but applies just as well to the formal constraints of a Google spreadsheet, which becomes part of a consciously designed workflow.

For an extreme example of designing workflows, consider the acclaimed independent game *POP: Methodology Experiment One*. In an interview, developer Rob Lach describes a similar experience as Mike Mika's, having worked on a larger game for over a year when the project fell apart due to lack of "momentum."[53] To regain his passion for making games, Lach decided to start by "remix[ing] the typical development pipeline," and he refers to the game as "what came out." This quote suggests a perspective in which the tools and content of the game become inextricably linked. Lach's own account of his work process indicates its performative quality, which is at odds with traditional views on game-making as a highly systematic, rationalized activity. For instance, he points to a scene in *POP* that was allegedly inspired by *Air Raid* (1982) and was "completely awful until the last hour of coding it when it all came together better than [he] expected." This episode more closely evokes a musician in the studio finally getting a decent take shortly before the recording studio closes than a programmer. And indeed, to create *POP*, Lach first created the music and then designed the gameplay experience "according to the emotive properties of that music."[54] He thus turned the development itself into a metagame, following the definition of philosopher Bernard Suits, who defines games as "goal-directed activities in which inefficient means are intentionally (or rationally) chosen" (Suits 1967, 148). This process may appear highly idiosyncratic, but a few other independent games, like *A Small Robot Story*, have already been developed using a similarly self-reflexive approach.[55] That is, while the unavoidable technical constraints on game-making are gradually eliminated, thereby reducing friction, developers feel compelled to impose their own restrictions instead.

This spectrum between technique and technology can also be observed in other media contexts. For instance, in the 1960s a French group of authors and mathematicians calling themselves OuLiPo sought to develop new forms of literature by devising and adhering to self-imposed rules (James 2009).[56] Simple rules operate as algorithms that produce quasi-random results; for instance, the S+7 principle allows for rewriting a text by replacing every noun with the seventh next entry in a dictionary.[57] Because the terms in the dictionary are not semantically related, the text becomes nonsensical; however, the overall sentence structure remains intact so that the text itself is still formally coherent. The more complex the constraints become, the more they resemble actual games. For instance, for his famous *Exercises in Style*, Raymond Queneau challenged himself to retell the same short story in ninety-nine ways, using established linguistic modes like reported speech or formal conventions like the haiku form as his rules of play. Put differently, the less formalized games appear as techniques, as variations of traditional literary practices, while the more formalized ones would instead be interpreted as tools in that they can be applied to different subject matters, require a well-defined input, and produce a (partially) predictable output.[58] The fact that OuLiPo devised games to support the writing process illustrates the fact that many tools, while not being designed for play, enable or even encourage forms of playfulness (Sicart 2014, 22). For instance, to create his hashbombs, Mike Mika playfully combined Twitter and his own game engine by defining a unique alphanumerical identifier for every currently running *#IDARB* match as a hashtag. Using the Twitter API, the game client could then search for new tweets referring to its game session and execute the corresponding hashbomb commands.

Finally, to further investigate how tools operate both as technique and technology, consider the case of sketching and doodling, which can serve to kill time but also trigger creative impulses. As a concept, it is not limited to pen and paper but also applies to interactive media. For instance, game engines like GameMaker: Studio are specifically tailored to sketching game ideas, such as by providing built-in functions for many common problems (e.g., collision detection or drawing) and by enabling developers to simply import objects from other game projects— that is, to reuse and repurpose earlier work. Freehand sketching is common in domains such as art (Menzel 1968), architecture (Suwa and Tversky 1996), and even literature (Byerly 1999). All these accounts, however, point to overlaps between material constraints and conventionalized activities. For instance, Menzel (1968) emphasizes how using a pen with waterproof ink affected his doodling style because it increased the "finality" (176) of each line. Finally, sketching and doodling are conceptually important because they connect the game developer's practice to the notion of authorship and the auteur. Even as early as 1928, German film director Friedrich Wilhelm Murnau described the camera as the "director's sketching pencil," which should be "as mobile as possible to catch every passing mood" (Koszarski 1990, 253). Digital prototyping and related techniques such as paper prototyping (Sefelin, Tscheligi, and Giller 2003) increasingly make this aspect of authorship, the hybrid status of sketches between artifact and practice, appear applicable to game-making as well.

Tool Use as Dialogue

"We shape our tools and then our tools shape us." Stemming from an article by John Culkin (1967), this quote is often misattributed to Marshall McLuhan and does indeed aptly summarize McLuhan's view on tools as technologies with media-like properties. Writing in the 1960s, Culkin mentions two phases, first the conception and then the widespread adoption of a new tool or technology. In times of digital media, however, these two phases occur much more quickly and regularly overlap because digital tools are continually updated, reshaped, sometimes split up, and recombined. This, in turn, implies a continuous quasi-dialogical relationship between user and tool.

Traditionally, technologies were considered either to determine their users' behavior (e.g., in the work of Karl Wittfogel and Walter Ong) or, inversely, to be determined by the social context of their construction (e.g., according to Wiebe Bijker and Trevor Pinch). The idea of a dialogue between tool and user implies a more nuanced view. For instance, office technologies are neither primarily social nor framed by material constraints but exhibit hybrid forms of use that Orlikowski (2007, 1435) calls "sociomaterial practices" but which can also be understood as a form of dialogue. This also applies to the use of sketches as outlined by Suwa and Tversky (1996). For instance, the authors report that architects "make unintended discoveries" (191) in their freehand drawings and describe this cyclical process as "like having a conversation with one's self" (191).

Apart from as a dialogue, the use of game design tools can similarly be described using the term *bricolage*, which refers to how making do with the resources available and strategically (re)combining them can be a way of unlocking one's creativity (see, e.g., Louridas 1999). For instance, developers creating a new game in Unity can choose to import several ready-made sample assets and scripts, such as characters, vehicles, and camera behavior such as a CCTV-style view.[59] Moreover, for many design tasks users already provide working snippets of code in online user forums, often with a backlog of posts that led to this approach, as well as alternative solutions. Making do with these existing building blocks is important especially for non-professional developers, who use and reuse them to formulate hypotheses and who receive answers by observing how they can or cannot be usefully incorporated into a game idea.

The notion of bricolage also demonstrates how games and tools increasingly converge. The joy of having to make do with limited resources similarly applies to games-as-tools like *Super Mario Maker* as many user-created levels stem from the self-imposed challenge to recreate gameplay patterns from genres other than platform games. For instance, the Ping Pong Battle level enables the player to control a "paddle" using a combination of bouncing blocks.[60] The rebounding ball is implemented via a shell and each shell the player misses first destroys one of three POW blocks (which symbolize three "lives") before activating a bomb dispenser that eliminates the playable Mario character.

The bricolage use of sample assets thus facilitates a continuous process of trial and error that appears dialogical and produces a

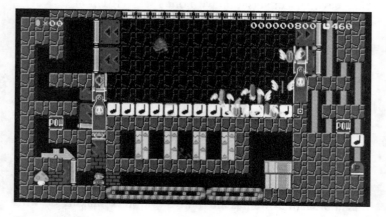

Figure 1.5
The Ping Pong Battle level in Super Mario Maker.

distinct rhetoric. Ian Bogost argues that playing a game creates a rhetorical situation not unlike the Socratic method (Bogost 2007, 15–17), in which a teacher asks seemingly open-ended questions (or the game affords different playing styles), accepts responses (or user input), and replies with a slightly modified version of that input (or the outcome of the player decision), thereby enabling the learner (or player) to observe their own assumptions and biases and to adapt their stance if necessary. The bricolage approach to game design creates a similar situation, and by providing a specific selection of sample assets, Unity is taking the role of Socrates, nudging the designer in a direction through corresponding (procedural) rhetoric.

The hypothesis that users enter a critical, quasi-dialogical relationship with their tools is substantiated by games in which the developers deliberately subvert the technological affordances they are presented with. For instance, consistent physics modeling is a property of many game engines that is highly naturalized and usually used in a naturalistic manner, to produce predictable movement within a simulated environment. The news game *The Cat and the Coup* (Peter Brinson and Kurosh ValaNejad, 2011), though, demonstrates an allegorical (see Owens 1980 on the use of allegory within postmodern aesthetics) use of physics modeling as the player impersonates an unlikely protagonist, the cat of Mohammed Mossadegh. The goal of the game is to push and topple objects to set the plot in motion—that is, to trigger key events in the narrative chronicling the CIA-engineered coup against the Iranian prime minister. Thus the physics simulation, a highly standardized and usually overlooked feature of many digital game worlds, acquires meaning in and of itself as the player must destabilize Mossadegh's environment to further the story. The increasingly chaotic scenes resulting from the

constant collision of numerous physics objects become a metaphor for the prime minister's psychological disposition, which
also appears jumbled. However, this development is not micro-
managed by the developers but essentially unscripted: it results
purely from the player's interaction with the physics system.[61]

From a production standpoint, this use of game tools can be
compared with the use of movie stars. In traditional Hollywood
cinema, the cultivation of stars, whose on-screen and off-screen
personas often became blurred, also followed the same rules
and became highly naturalized, less noticeable to viewers as a
deliberate construction. Because of that, though, movie stars in
neonoir films were often cast in roles that played off of and subverted their public appearance (Silver 1996, 334–335). Physics
routines in games are partially comparable to actors in that they
are usually licensed and that creators want to get their money's worth. Thus, like the physics simulation in *The Cat and the
Coup*, famous actors in neonoir films cannot simply be taken for
granted; they add meaning by creating and subverting expectations and are tools that enable complex, quasi-dialogical forms
of use.

An Operational Aesthetic of Digital Games

Finally, sketching a production studies perspective of digital
games also requires considering the perspective of the users/
players. As in the case of film and television before, the creation
of games is becoming more and more transparent. Accessible
tools like ScratchJr and Code.org use game and play elements to
foster algorithmic literacy among children and, in the process,
also provide an abstracted glimpse into the making of a digital
game. An important implication of the increasing production
awareness in contemporary American television, caused by

thematic redundancies and the reuse of familiar story tropes, is the fact that viewers come to appreciate fictional programs more for their operational achievements—for example, juggling multiple storylines and "narrative spectacle[s]" (Mittell 2006, 36) such as musical episodes—than for what is actually happening in the story. Jason Mittell has described this shift of perspective using the term *operational aesthetics* (35). This section argues that the same perspective shift is also gradually adopted by gamers.

The multiplicity of currently available game-making tools leads to a similar abundance of digital games that readjust player perceptions to focus on how a specific effect was implemented rather than what happens in the game's narrative. Players gradually learn how hard it is to make commercial games and that there are still complete polished games being made by one person.[62] They interpret games through the lens of tools—for instance, through modding (Sotamaa 2010), which has become an increasingly common practice, not least due to the success of games like *Super Mario Maker* (2016). Yet they also reappropriate games as tools for self-expression—for instance, in the case of game designer and critic Greg Loring-Albright, who modified the popular board game Settlers of Catan to critique instances of bias in the original design, which allegedly casts players in the role of colonizers without confronting them with the consequences of occupying a potentially inhabited territory (Loring-Albright 2015). Game-making has even recently become the plot of other narrative media, including manga and anime such as *Saenai Heroine No Sodatekata* (2012–) and *Shoujo-tachi wa Kouya o Mezasu* (2016–). The protagonists in these stories are young, Japanese, independent (or *doujin*) game developers, which makes the process and the tools they use relatable not only on a technical but also on an empathetic level.[63]

In response to shifting viewer perceptions, television formats adapted over time, developing more "complex" (Mittell 2006, 30) and more self-reflexive or "self-conscious" (34) modes of storytelling. These new types of stories acknowledge the increased production knowledge of the viewers and challenge them to continually readjust and expand their mental models. Accordingly, scripted reality shows like *Survivor* appear "more like a horse race than fiction" (Jenkins 2009, 28), and both fans trying to spoil the show (by reverse-engineering its production context) and counterfans "spoiling the *Survivor* spoilers" expressly describe their engagement with television as a "game" (49). Similarly, independent games have recently begun to play with their own workflows as a means of playing (or toying) with the players' operational aesthetics, systematically overstraining their expectations. For instance, *Fez* (2012) invented a symbolic spatial unit called *triles/trixels* to represent its noncontiguous play space, *Antichamber* (2013) utilizes regular-looking but non-Euclidean geometry with impossible objects, and the developers of *Miegakure* (2016) resorted to a proxy concept based on Edwin Abbott Abbott's novel *Flatland* (1884) to simulate a four-dimensional game world.[64]

These games assume that players have basic knowledge of how games normally work and tweak their tools to upend these expectations. In the three games just mentioned, the developers consequently documented the production process very thoroughly before release to facilitate this asynchronous dialogue with the players, allowing them to catch up and develop new playing strategies. Finally, like Mittell's observations on television, operational aesthetics in the context of games allows for new angles of appreciating clever production techniques (i.e., "marvel[ing] at how far creators can push the boundaries of complexity"; cf. Mittell 2006, 35). For instance, the prominent Kickstarter-funded *Wasteland 2* was initially viewed skeptically because the developers publicly stated that they were buying many assets from the Unity Asset Store rather than creating them in-house. However, after release, players praised developer inXile Entertainment for recombining the assets in creative ways and juxtaposing them with content crowdsourced from the user community, thereby pioneering new forms of consumer-producer relationships.[65] As these examples demonstrate, the increasing technical diversification and sophistication of game creation tools exhibits a trickle-down effect, gradually entering the collective player experience and readjusting the players' perception of a game, similar to how TV viewers have learned to appreciate the craftsmanship of complex television narratives and to substitute empathetic immersion in a plot with intellectual immersion in television as a broader cultural phenomenon.

Following the initial example of *#IDARB*, chapter 2 aims to refine the conceptual framework outlined in this chapter by considering additional case studies and inferring more specific concepts for the purpose of tool criticism. Despite the diversity of cases, they all reaffirm the direct connection between playing and making games. This mindset is common in earlier forms of play, such as in the case of children blurring the boundaries between playing games, consensually modifying the rules to suit their playing style, and creating new games altogether, but many of us lose it as adults. In that sense, tools are instrumental in bridging a technology-induced gap between game players and game designers. Therefore, chapter 3 will conclude the book by unpacking why and how game creation tools need to become more evocative, thus enabling us to consider games not just as products but as a form of expression and reflection.

2 Tool Essays: From Tool Fandom and Aesthetic Ecosystems to the Evolution of Tool Affordances

This chapter presents a series of short, self-contained *tool essays*, most of which focus on one phenomenon and a corresponding generalizable trait or concept that can be applied to other types of (digital) tools as well. For instance, software tools increasingly adapt and reinterpret functionality established earlier in a different context, attempting to reconcile those features with their own, more contemporary purposes. With regard to new media, Jay David Bolter and Richard Grusin call this process *remediation*, arguing that "every new medium diverges from yet also reproduces older media, whereas old media refashion themselves to answer the challenges of new media" (Deuze 2006, 68). For instance, websites initially recreated and experimented with (i.e., remediated) the aesthetics of newspaper cover pages or posters.

Buildbox, a drag-and-drop tool developed in 2014 specifically to create "hypercasual games" for mobile devices, breaks projects down into multiple *scenes*, a term that references clips in video editing and compositing applications like Adobe Premiere or After Effects and applies that concept to game levels.[1] More uniquely, though, to play only one particular scene, users can "solo" that scene by pressing the S key.[2] This concept is "imported" from the playback functionality of multitrack music software like Sibelius or Logic Pro, where "soloing" a voice temporarily mutes all other voices. In that sense, the Buildbox feature can be regarded as remediating much older music software functionality. Similar processes of remediation also can be found in other tools. For instance, the web-based music sequencer *turtle.audio* employs a visual interface that enables users to create music by drawing paths and positioning black dots that follow the paths and produce sounds along the way.[3] The system explicitly remediates the popular 1980s educational programming language Logo and its "turtle graphics" principle, which creates images by moving a relative cursor, the "turtle," upon a Cartesian plane.

By exploring one concept in each section, this chapter expounds on how tools, much like games themselves, should be interpreted as designed objects with a "procedural rhetoric" (Bogost 2008, 125) of their own. Just as proceduralist readings (Treanor and Mateas 2011) foreground gameplay elements that are meaningful and unusual, the chapter emphasizes unusual or evocative design features with distinct rhetorical qualities.

Procedural Rhetoric and Metaphors of Control in Planning Tools

In a chapter on the design tools provided with *Second Life* (2003–), Shenja van der Graaf (2017) describes the individual functions that allow users to "produce houses, mountains and so forth that can be shared, moved, copied and sold" (94). Functional limitations are hereby primarily interpreted as a "nuisance" (96), and episodic quotes from *Second Life* users seem to substantiate this limited view. It is true that "the built-in toolkit conditions the creative space for internal mod development" (97), but the more interesting question is: How? Neither tools to create games nor those to manage the creation process are ever neutral, but to assess their procedural rhetoric, it is important to know what to look for. Content and progression charts are useful to illustrate this point; they are created using tools but also constitute tools in themselves and are often designed to appear objective and comprehensive. For instance, in her 2018 GDC talk, game designer Jennifer Scheurle refers to a particularly detailed example created by Jean Guesdon in Adobe Illustrator for the game *Assassin's Creed 2*; she also discussed this example on Twitter.[4]

The chart maps the co-occurrence of story moments, racing elements, tutorials, and assassinations throughout the game. For that purpose, even though games are inherently nonlinear, the chart establishes the notion of *beats*, moments during gameplay that are organized chronologically in terms of when they occur in relation to one another.

One would expect this timeline visualization in the context of cinema to be a primarily time-based medium, and indeed the

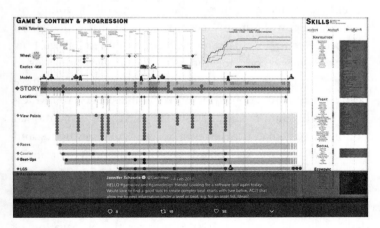

Figure 2.1
Beat diagram for Assassin's Creed 2, from Jennifer Scheurle's Twitter feed.

visualization exhibits striking similarities to an earlier type of diagram, the vertical montage charts created by Sergei Eisenstein for his historical epos *Alexander Nevsky* (1938; see Smith 2014, 89). Eisenstein's charts most importantly document—and thereby also organize—the correlation of music and image. Only parts of Sergei Prokofiev's film score were composed to existing footage; indeed, several sections of the film were deliberately edited to match previously written and recorded music. By visually combining a piano reduction of the score with diagrams of pictorial composition and on-screen movement, synchronicity—in the form of gradual upward movement—was easy to identify and, therefore, felt particularly "natural" to implement as well.

Both Eisenstein's and Guesdon's diagrams operate as *boundary objects* (as defined in chapter 1); that is, they enable collaboration and facilitate discussion between groups of people, for whom concepts like audiovisual synchronicity might otherwise mean very different things. According to Alan Galey and Stan Ruecker, a designed prototype can "argue" (405), communicate meaning, without any accompanying textual explanation; similarly, Eisenstein's diagrams reify his hypotheses about how music and images come together in the language of film. Due to its visual similarities with Eisenstein's visualizations, which have been subsequently adopted by other filmmakers as well, Guesdon's beat diagram can be understood using the aforementioned notion of remediation. However, its particular aesthetics and visual similarities to dashboards also suggest a different angle: the attempt to visualize data to create a semblance of control over complex, often unruly systems (like the messiness of potential ways to play a game). In his influential commentary on city dashboards, Michael Batty (2015) assesses the propagation of dashboard visualizations in contemporary culture, positing a

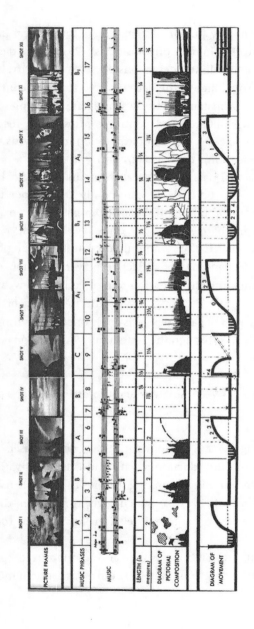

Figure 2.2

Diagram used in the filming of Alexander Nevsky (1938), (https://commons.wikimedia.org/wiki/File:Vertical_montage_Eisenstein._1st_part_of_ex..jpg).

shift from "monitoring human systems" (e.g., for medical purposes) to "monitoring human organizations" (29). Batty's dashboards focus on controlling interactions of systems in a city, but the argument also applies to the decentralized forms of control in game design. For instance, Batty warns against the "present obsession with dash-boards and control centres" (30), fueled by the desire to make sense of complex (social) interactions via readily available real-time data visualization.

Contrary to actual dashboards, beat diagrams are static, but they are intended to be updated continually throughout the creation process, incorporating feedback from playtesting experiences and design changes. In social game development, real-time dashboards are actually commonly used and thus tangibly shape users' understandings of collective player behavior. For instance, by comparing the retention rate of current, new, and reactivated users and correlating it with the frequency of in-game deaths, the goal of game design is envisioned as ensuring a constant flow of users through the system, moving at a constant and steady pace.[5]

Bridging the Gap between Amateur and Professional Game Creators

Ideally, tool design ensures a similarly steady flow of users by providing a smooth introduction, creating intrinsic motivation to remain engaged, and incorporating features that enable users to develop and test their skills, which, over time, alters their identities as game creators and their relationships with the tools themselves.

In that regard, tutorial projects play an important role, serving as a gateway into a tool and providing basic orientation.

Ann-Sophie Lehmann (2012) illustrates how ready-made content can instill a sense of shared identity in a community of creators by retracing the history of the Utah teapot, a 3-D model built using Bezier curves rather than polygons, which, "because the dataset . . . was small and freely available, . . . became the logical test bed for new rendering algorithms" (174) after its creation in 1974. The 3-D object was perceived as a self-imposed challenge from and for the 3-D graphics community, aiming to "move emerging 3D computer graphics from spheres and cubes into the domain of recognizable, real-life things" (173). It can be interpreted as a tool with its own procedural rhetoric: features like "complex topology, . . . self-shadows, . . . hidden surface issues [and] both convex and concave surfaces" (174). This made it interesting and challenging to work and play with, which added to its iconicity. This example can be easily adapted to more recent tools, such as the sample datasets provided by popular data visualization tool Gephi.[6] Gephi is primarily used for producing network visualizations using force-directed graphs, and the sample datasets constitute a distinct set of affordances that nonverbally define what, according to Gephi, a (social) network is (i.e., its ontology). Apart from the expected datasets on professional and private, online and offline social networks, from Perl developers to Jazz musicians to Twitter users, the samples also include data from fictional contexts, such as characters from *Les Misérables* or Marvel superheroes. Thus, the sample projects constitute an entry point that frames using Gephi as more than just as a frictionless but also fun and, through its tongue-in-cheek humor, self-reflexive process.

The film sample project for Unity, added in late 2018, is a game-specific example with interesting procedural rhetorical characteristics, which entices users to try creating cinematic sequences in the engine.[7] Moreover, Unity provides a subway tunnel scene as a playground to experiment with dynamic lighting and materials, to "set . . . up a good baseline for believable visuals."[8] In contrast, the early demos for GameMaker 1.4 comprised clones of iconic casual games like *Angry Birds* (2009) and *Fruit Ninja* (2010). These projects demonstrated technical features like 2-D physics and swipe controls, but also procedurally framed recreating and modifying commercially successful games as the "preferred" way to become a game developer.

Although sample projects are a common tool design element, GameMaker is one of the few tools that include software affordances to deliberately modulate the transition from amateur to (semi)professional. Previous ethnographic work on professional (O'Donnell 2014; van der Graaf 2012) and independent (Guevara-Villalobos 2011; Nieborg and Van der Graaf 2008)

Figure 2.3
GameMaker 1.4 demos (https://help.yoyogames.com/hc/en-us/articles /217571368-Download-Studio-1-4-Demos-And-Tutorials).

game production suggests marked differences in these different cultures. Therefore, GameMaker is relevant as a potential bridge between these worlds, which allowed developers like Jonatan Söderström (*Hotline Miami*) and Derek Yu (*Spelunky*) to carve out a niche for themselves in the game industry.

Most importantly, it offers both a drag-and-drop visual scripting system seen in many entry-level tools like the MIT-developed Scratch or App Inventor and a more traditional scripting language called Geography Markup Language (GML). Moreover, GameMaker rhetorically links both systems because drag-and-drop actions can be viewed as actual GML code.[9] Changing drag-and-drop actions directly modifies the corresponding code, even though the inverse is not possible. This affords at least one-way transcoding between the amateur and the professional system, marking both spheres as permeable, making the possibility to transition from one to the other appear almost tangible.

Moreover, GameMaker offers built-in functions that take over routine programming tasks like transforming an angle and distance into a vector (lengthdir_x/y) or finding the nearest enemy (instance_nearest). These are useful for beginners, and discarding them later marks a rite of passage within the user's creator identity. These code snippets operate like LEGO bricks, and GameMaker, unlike many other engines, also offers bigger but less flexible pieces, such as dedicated functions for drawing a health bar or high score list, which can later be replaced and customized. To keep the construction from collapsing, Game-Maker, like LEGO, offers predefined connections between pieces, like inferring variable types or deleting temporary constructs to prevent memory leaks.

Thus, GameMaker can be conceptualized by Sherry Turkle (2007) as a *liminal object* (8) because its continued use marks a transition, often imperceptible from moment to moment and from player to maker. The same applies also, for example, to the use of homebrew tools among Nintendo DS grassroots developers. O'Donnell (2014) analyzes the motivations fueling these communities, but also points out how their ethos clashes with Nintendo's legal efforts to curtail the distribution of hardware and software to create independent DS games. In this context, homebrew tools are liminal objects because they allow for running one's own game on the iconically closed Nintendo hardware.[10] This shift of perspective might be considered similar to the fascination of early gaming hardware developers like Ralph Baer with controlling even simple shapes on a television screen via early consoles, for which Baer distinctly uses the term *TV games* as opposed to *videogames*.[11]

Moving beyond individual tools, developing a shared vocabulary within the game industry over time is effectively shaping language into a tool for constituting and continually reaffirming a *professional game industry culture* (and learning that language can be a tool to immerse in it). For instance, Neil Katharine (2012) quotes game designer Doug Church's claim that the lack of a "common vocabulary of terms to describe game concepts" constitutes a major hurdle in "pass[ing] down and build[ing] upon knowledge from generation to generation of game designers" (6). Church's comments date back to 1999, but Tracy Fullerton expressed a similar sentiment in 2008, calling the lack of a shared vocabulary "one of the largest problems facing the game industry today" (qtd. in Katharine 2012, 6). Yet adopting and routinely using specialized terminology is not just a tool for knowledge transfer; it also has a performative dimension: it can be a prop in transitioning through roleplay from the part of the amateur to that of a (semi)professional. A discussion on the GameMaker forums on the notion of "game feel" illustrates this point, as discussants use this flexible but seemingly clear-cut term as a boundary object in discussions to perform their own identity as "serious" game designers, as well as their adherence to that community.[12]

Tool Fandom

As indicated in chapter 1, large companies have increasingly been sharing their tools to attract talent instead of black-boxing the internal production process. Apart from Disney's aforementioned Ptex, one of the most prominent gaming examples is the free-to-use PhyreEngine, launched by Sony Interactive Entertainment in 2008 to facilitate making games for the PlayStation 3, which was difficult to utilize properly due to its Cell Broadband Engine Architecture.[13] Arguably, this strategy reflects an epistemic shift, indicating that companies begin to perceive their tools more as a service, which becomes more valuable through sharing, than as a product, which has to be kept scarce to maintain its value.

From a media and culture studies perspective, this strategy can be explained as an attempt to stimulate *tool fandom*. That is, in a best-case scenario, it would provide aspiring developers not only with know-how but also with the cognitive gratification and social recognition that come from identifying with the company as a franchise and from using their tools with a fan mindset. This section explores how fan studies can help us understand the precarious balance between external influence and bottom-up affective engagement that characterizes both fan identities and communities and the relation between users, tools, and platforms.

Fandom is often an inherently social process, as illustrated, for example, in Henry Jenkins's analysis of a *Survivor* spoiler fan community (Jenkins 2006, 25–58), and the same also often applies to tool use. For instance, in the context of amateur game design, Peppler and Kafai (2007) identified the formation of communities around entry-level tools such as Bryce and Scratch. In these communities, the joint learning experience and collective acquisition of media literacy, as well as engagement in a thriving participatory culture, were the main drivers. Similarly, in game modding communities, which usually comprise both amateur and semiprofessional creators, being part of a tool community— that is, a shared "computer game modding culture" (Sotamaa 2010, 239)—constitutes one primary motivation. Sotamaa's ethnographic work provides hints at how material affordances foster that sense of group identity. For instance, ID Software's *Doom* (1993), one of the oldest moddable games with a still-active community, stored its media files separately, which "supported the emergence of specified skills and division of modders into different roles" (Sotamaa 2010, 245), thus structuring the community and facilitating its organic growth. Even the "very limited" documentation, due to which "most of the learning takes place through trial and error" (247) and by sharing tidbits of information, can be regarded as a sociotechnical mechanism (see "#IDARB and the Many Sides of Game Tools" in chapter 1) that promotes a social game creation experience.

All these social interactions contribute not just to the accumulation of "gaming capital" (Sotamaa 2010, 243)—that is, social recognition within a gaming community—but also to the accumulation of social capital in corresponding tool communities. This process is similar to what, with reference to sports fandom, Sturm and McKinney (2013) call *fan capital*, the negotiation of "status, prestige, authority, value, skills, tastes and knowledge." Robert Nideffer paints a more pessimistic picture of game creation as a social process (Nideffer 2011). He defines game engines as "creative frameworks" (175), and "explor[es] how the contexts within which these tools emerge can themselves function as an 'engine'" (176). Yet Nideffer calls these contexts a "corporate engine . . . predicated upon efficient institutional reproduction through habitually patterned behavior and product in as unproblematic a way as possible." His main focus is on how media artists use and appropriate game engines, and from that angle, the corporate engine appears "diametrically opposed" (176) to the goals and practices of artists. Nideffer claims that game engines force users into repetitive behavior ("patterned repetition of the acts of individual agents"; 180), which—according to Giddens's structuration theory—reproduces deeper corresponding social structures. This perspective is rather normative and positions media artists' appropriation of tools as a go-to solution to break that alleged cycle. Instead, the link to fandom, which acknowledges both compulsive and empowered forms of fan participation, might afford a more open-ended discussion about tool engagement.

One way to operationalize tool fandom as a concept is to compare Jenkins's observations on media "fans' investment in the aired material" (Jenkins 2006, 57) with the investment in a tool. This rhetoric comes back repeatedly; for instance, Jenkins distinguishes among "emotional, social, and intellectual investments" (63) and argues that fans are likely to "protect . . . their investments in [a] series" (21). All this also applies, for example, to iconic older tools like the Build engine, developed by Ken Silverman in 1995, which became famous for its use in *Duke Nukem 3D* (1996). Build was recently reactivated by tool fans, who founded Voidpoint to release their own fork of the engine called EDuke32 and create the shooter game *Ion Maiden* (2019).[14] By modding old Build games like *Blood* (1997), fans had continuously invested effort into learning the tool, similar to how fans drill deeper into the backstory of their franchise of choice to become more adept, for example, at formulating or assessing fan theories. Build fans also invested time in forming a community and stand to lose that "fan capital" if their community were to disappear. In this case, tool fandom of the game engine and fandom of *Duke Nukem 3D* as a generation-defining first-person shooter became inextricably linked.

Structural similarities with religious practice constitute a second useful point of comparison between media and tool fandom. Jenkins (2006) argues that the narrative structure of fan-favorite franchises is the "'monomyth,' a conceptual structure abstracted from a cross-cultural analysis of the world's great religions" (120), and that diverging opinions can "lead to religious wars among fans" (162). Moreover, concepts like *canonicity*—the selection of "authoritative" texts—and *exegesis*—assigning the role of interpreting and explaining these texts to a select group of people—are intuitively applied in many fan contexts. These categories also apply to tool fandom. Large software tool companies like Adobe and Autodesk even frame their influencers as *tool evangelists*.[15] For instance, sound engineer Jason Levine is explicitly called Adobe Jesus by his followers, and his demonstrations of new software features can be interpreted as akin to performing miracles to spread the good word.[16]

Rivalries between franchises (e.g., *Star Wars* vs. *Star Trek*) and between tools constitute yet another productive approach to put the notion of tool fandom into practice. In a forum discussion on Construct 2 versus GameMaker: Studio, users critically debate the implied notion of tool fandom in general.[17] For instance, an anonymous guest user argues: "i don't really have any special attachment to Gamemaker, but i don't generally form attachments with tools in general." These rivalries are culturally rooted in the sometimes good-natured but often highly entrenched oppositions between fan communities of sports teams, one of the earliest forms of fan identity conflicts related to games. For instance, Benkwitz and Molnar (2012) position "football rivalries within the broader genre of fandom" and characterize these symbolic conflicts that allow for performing fandom as "unique and complex [phenomena], underpinned by social, historical and/or cultural factors" (479).

Finally, even though tool fandom, much like media fandom, is often an inherently social phenomenon, it can also manifest itself in individual use. As we incorporate software tools into our everyday habits (as media fans do with their favorite franchises), they become part of our day-to-day identity performance, both in professional and private contexts. For instance, McMillan (2013) documents how GitHub, a tool originally designed for collaborative software development, is being used for everything from planning weddings to curating a compendium of Gregorian chants. That is, users internalize the distinct "style of cooperative tinkering" they identify with the tool and apply it as a filter to interpret everyday life, similar to how, say, *Game of Thrones* fans interpreted the 2016 election through the lens of the popular HBO show's lore.[18]

These examples demonstrate the affective qualities of using tools. Anthony Chemero draws on Martin Heidegger's philosophical understanding of tools to argue that a "tool isn't separate from you it's part of you" (qtd. in Keim 2010). Similar to the GitHub users discussed earlier, independent developer Evan

Todd, outlining the design of his node/based dialogue tree tool at the Game Developers Conference (GDC) in 2016, states that his "development philosophy . . . actually extends beyond game development into other aspects of life."[19] This affective engagement can be channeled through routine practices of tool fandom and use such as customizing, organizing, and displaying them. For instance, in a video tour of his workshop, engineer and bricoleur Adam Savage outlines his approach to organizing tools using custom storage stands, which clearly reflects a set of general guiding principles, such as how to keep only the important things in view at all times.[20] In a different video on toolboxes, Savage hints at the affective quality of these practices, admitting to "deeply love and [be] comforted by extreme levels of organization."[21]

The sense of personal accomplishment and gratification that sustains tool fan identity can also be traced in game industry rhetoric and is often tied to the procedural rhetoric of the tools involved. In his 2014 GDC talk on *Rayman Legends*, level designer Chris McEntee argues that "the secret to designing Rayman is actually quite similar to the secret of playing Rayman, which is rapid iterative failure."[22] McEntee continues: "You fail about 40 times a day but then you get one win before you go home for the night," a sentiment that is immediately familiar to many gamers. Further into the talk, McEntee talks about the possibility of discovering new and unexpected aspects in UbiArt, the design framework used to create the more recent *Rayman* games: "What's really interesting is sometimes when you go exploring in areas of an engine that you're not supposed to touch you find out that it actually has something to bring to your job." These surprising but rewarding findings directly cater to the principles of "drillability" and "extractability" (qtd. in Bourdaa 2013, 208), which Henry Jenkins identified as pillars of transmedia fandom. They afford an embodied experience and personal engagement beyond merely fulfilling a practical purpose.

Bricolage: From Aesthetic Ecosystems to the Playful Appropriation of Tools

In a 2005 article, Diomidis Spinellis reports on his own experiments with creating stand-alone, interoperable software tools, which compel him to call *tool writing*—that is, the creation of dedicated software tools for (at least initially) personal use—a "forgotten art" (Spinellis 2005). This rhetoric evokes the craftsman creating or at least fine-tuning and appropriating the tools of their trade and designing auxiliary constructs for specific purposes as needed.

A similar argument can be made by looking at the early days of digital game production, when teams were smaller and developers created their own tools with all their quirks and idiosyncrasies. Anita Sinclair, a programmer at Magnetic Scrolls and creator of several highly innovative text-graphic adventures like *The Pawn* (1986) and *Wonderland* (1990), revealed in a 1987 interview that her team created all tools, including a compiler and a unique programming language to create adventure game parsers, by itself.[23] Sinclair's main reason was similar to that a physical craftsman might give—namely, that building and fine-tuning tools is the only way to ensure their reliability and thus is part of their own professional ethos.

Instead, appropriating and recombining existing tools is much more common in game creation today. This form of bricolage (as defined in chapter 1) or tinkering manifests itself particularly clearly in online asset marketplaces like the Unity

Asset Store.[24] In terms of procedural rhetoric, creating an economy for game assets in itself frames digital games as collections
of parts rather than an integral whole, as players begin to find
the same 3-D model or postprocessing shader in multiple games.
The ordering and filtering categories of the Unity Asset Store
concretize that procedural rhetoric. For instance, all code assets
that are not visual effects or add-ons are internally labeled *tools*,
yet labels can change over time depending on which assets are
popular. The visual effects category comprises both shaders and
particle effects, yet one of only three sections in the latter category is dedicated to magical spell effects. To explain this rather
specific choice, it is important to know that the Unity Asset Store
places disproportionate emphasis on successful "products." On
the launch page, "top grossing packages" are displayed at the top
of the list, and all subcategories in each section are ordered by
"best selling assets" by default.

Due to this market logic, which gives already popular assets
more exposure and thus favors oligopolistic structures, the Unity
Asset Store can best be understood as an aesthetic ecosystem.
That ecosystem offers niches for particular types of content to
thrive in, and even allows for symbiotic effects (e.g., as creators
produce content complementary to existing popular assets). The
term *aesthetic ecosystem* is derived from the notion of an "economic ecosystem" (Rosmarin 2006), which journalist and author
Rachel Rosmarin coined to emphasize how early platforms like
Myspace, through their sheer size, created niches for other developers to develop functions that users wanted to see in an online
social network but that the developers did not anticipate. In the
context of the Unity Asset Store, this process of natural selection
among game assets and the bricolage design practices it affords
tangibly shape and potentially constrain game aesthetics.

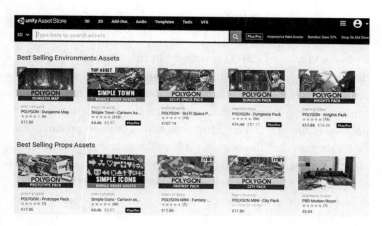

Figure 2.4
The Unity Asset Store.

For instance, the top selling 3-D environments (as of April 2019) comprise cartoon-style, low-poly props for fantasy and science fiction settings. Such clearly identifiable clichés do not apply in all cases, though. For example, the top-level editing script exhibits multiple patterns, particularly splines (i.e., soft curves), but also tile-mapping, voxels, and the physics-based scattering of decal objects in a level.[25] Yet, through repetition, these patterns and the iconicity of the assets that represent them usually increases further.

As earlier production studies have shown, the availability of material to choose from has usually depended on social networks. For instance, Sullivan (2009) draws on the work of Leo C. Rosten to point out how Hollywood operated as a "social system" (45) characterized by both formal and informal ties, which ultimately shaped film aesthetics. Rosten writes in and about the 1940s, yet the talents and assets that are available for a specific production still often depend on the contacts and collaboration opportunities of the producers involved. The social systems that Guevara-Villalobos (2011) identified in the context of independent game production fulfill similar purposes, but, by and large, online marketplaces are taking over some of these functions of informal social systems in terms of structuring the production process (Chapple 2012). This can make smaller productions easier to plan and finance, but it also has a few important side effects. To counter the framing effect of prebuilt assets—that is, to avoid building a new game around existing material—developers sometimes devise new ways of incorporating asset stores into their workflows. For instance, for the development of *Wasteland 2* (2014), inXile Entertainment combined assets purchased on the Unity Asset Store with a crowdsourcing experiment.[26] They offered modelers an art guide and a list of required assets but, most importantly, allowed them to retain the rights to their assets and to keep selling them on the UAS and to reference their Wasteland 2 production credits if selected. Thus, rather than simply using the Unity Asset Store, the developer co-opted and codesigned an aesthetic ecosystem. Existing material, from asset stores or otherwise, can also afford creative challenges in deliberate bricolage practices. The postmortem for *Half-Life* (1998) points to such a situation in a professional production context (Birdwell 1999). In that case, the designers recombined existing set pieces, props, and behaviors that had been created early in the development of *Half-Life* but did not coalesce into a convincing whole. The team formulated self-imposed rules of play, such as trying to combine seemingly incompatible assets in creative ways—which, according to the postmortem, allowed a fresh take on familiar design problems and inspired some of the gameplay elements for which the *Half-Life* franchise would later become famous.

Yet more often than not, minimizing friction by making it as seamless as possible to find and import external assets can be harmful to game-making as a creative process because it incentivizes reactive and nonreflective use. While inconvenient, irritations and even roadblocks in game creation can act as productive constraints that require designers-as-players to find creative workarounds, which is why minimizing these constraints can limit the design imaginary. For instance, commonly available lens flare effects are found in many amateur games, usually in a somewhat naturalistic way aimed at imitating the aesthetics of commercial bigger-budget games.[27] The lens flares are usually parametrizable, but the overall ease of use and built-in defaults often discourage developers from using the parameters—and the effect itself—in unforeseen and expressive ways. Instead, the abundance of similar-looking lens flares in digital games constrains the semantic potential of this stylistic device and primarily reaffirms its existing connotations, such as evoking a generically cinematic look. Mike Bithell, creator of indie surprise hit *Thomas Was Alone* (2012), expresses a similar sentiment. On the Unity Technologies Blog, he argues that "things like rendering a silhouette when the player moves behind an obstacle, or handling palette swapping characters" had to be developed anew and thus reconsidered for every new game but now become readily available tools in themselves.[28] Revisiting the Heideggerian terminology from the previous section on tool fandom, they are "ready-to-hand" (Keim 2010); that is, we use them—like a hammer—without thinking, or, more specifically, we are thinking through them about the problem at hand.

A critical exercise to help minimize that often unavoidable problem might be to consider ready-made assets in the tradition of found footage, in the artistic sense as détournement or with reference to more contemporary digital video remixing practices

(Horwatt 2009). Remixing digital video footage, according to Horwatt, is a "continuation in the development of the strategies and techniques of found footage filmmaking but possesses its own unique aesthetic and rhetorical contributions" (76). Accordingly, found footage films, both in 1920s/1930s avantgarde cinema and today, often combine material with a critical purpose, such as in the form of "estrangement" and defamiliarization, "politicized recalibration or inversion" (77). Adapting appropriative strategies from these earlier media contexts can help overcome the logic of reconciliation and gradual improvement that characterizes common asset reuse practices in game creation.

While most game creators do not "make" their own tools, asset markets enable them to at least customize their game engines as a means of perfecting them and making them their own, thus expressing themselves through the tool and practicing tool fandom as suggested in the previous section. For instance, users of GameMaker: Studio, which does not support video playback out of the box, have been discussing extensively their wish for developer YoYo Games to incorporate one of several video plugins available on the GameMaker Marketplace into the tool itself to "complete" it. Moreover, some assets offer functionality that already exists in the engine but implement it in a different, often arguably more efficient or economical manner. For instance, the Custom Sprite Framework aims to fix the "terrible performance issues due to hundreds or sometimes even thousands of texture swaps" in GameMaker using the existing sprite-related functions.[29] Other assets like Custom Draw Text simply add to the existing functionality (in this case, text drawing).[30] Both creating and choosing to use these "redundant" functions over the existing ones customizes the tool and, in the process, allows users to communicate their own viewpoint on how it should work.

Apart from tinkering with assets explicitly offered for bricolage work, game creators also appropriate existing tools by taking
them out of their original context. For instance, Digital Dreams's
Roy van de Mortel repurposed Microsoft Excel and Word as ana-
lytics tools to optimize puzzle placement for *Metrico* (2014).[31]
First, van de Mortel would visualize the complexity of puzzles in
Word by combining a screenshot with a grid-like overview of the
puzzle's characteristics. To create the grid, he turned the Affect
Grid, a psychological heuristic meant to qualify "judgments
about affect of either a descriptive or a subjective kind," into a
tool by translating it into Word's table functionality.[32] Then he
created a difficulty tier system for the puzzles, added the difficul-
ties of all puzzles planned for each world in Excel, and used con-
ditional formatting to quickly visualize, using colors from green
to red, and compare the aggregate difficulty against predefined
thresholds. This process, which van de Mortel tellingly calls "a
puzzle in itself," was intended to ensure a smooth increase in
difficulty. Robert Yang's *Hurt Me Plenty* can help illustrate how
features of actual game creation tools, in this case the ragdoll
physics implementation in Unity, can be appropriated.[33] Yang,
an assistant arts professor at the NYU Game Center, felt that for
his self-described gay spanking simulator, "canned animation
seemed too rigid" to communicate the difference between pain
and abuse in the context of light BDSM. Traditionally, ragdoll
physics are used "for 'realistically' falling down a mountain, getting hit by a car, or dying in a dramatic fashion by flopping
over a railing"; according to Yang, "it's for when people die,"
whereas he wanted to use it to "simulate life." Thus, Yang "glued
the submissive's knees and hands to the ground, where they
act as hinges," and to keep the model upright, he "attached a
small invisible jet engine below his chest." By repurposing and

tweaking these two preexisting functions, he aimed to convey bodily reactions of the in-game character, such as "breathing heavily or losing his balance." Thus, combining two physics systems and using them in a nonstandard manner allowed Yang to tentatively push beyond binary representations in games, wherein a specific animation is either playing or not, and to reflect on the contingencies of virtual bodies in games.

In his cognitive analysis of tool appropriation, Salovaara (2008) indicates a "lack of studies that would have documented appropriations systematically" (215), indicating that more examples like the ones just discussed will be necessary to understand this common but often marginalized process better. Finally, as game creation is slowly but steadily becoming more pervasive and more people adopt a game designer's perspective in their use of digital media, games can become tools themselves. The player-created "games" in *Habbo* (2000–) serve to illustrate this point. For instance, the Fridge Game is built around and repurposes the random item distribution of the Pura Refrigerator item in *Habbo*.[34] Players take turns taking items out of the fridge and, depending on the found item, can stay in the game, make another player leave the game, or have to leave themselves. Thus, the game's creators and players reenvision *Habbo*'s functionality with a bricolage mindset to enrich social interaction on the platform. They enable players to create a shared "micronarrative" (Bizzocchi 2007, 7) through the game or to win recognition in the game's virtual community. They can also afford social catharsis, such as by enabling a group to kick unsociable or even hostile players out according to the game's rules. This form of tinkering with *Habbo* is playful on several levels. *Playfulness* is a commonly used term, but Miguel Sicart defines it specifically as a "way of engaging with the world derived from our capacity to play but lacking some of the characteristics of play" (Sicart 2014, 21). Accordingly, a playful disposition allows us to "see how the world could be structured as play" (25), that is—with regard to *Habbo*—how social media can afford forms of play that forego the rather blatant and commodified rhetoric of play adopted by platforms like Instagram or Snapchat.

Tools and the Changing Ontology of Digital Game Worlds

Investigating tools can be a powerful strategy to better understand developments within the field of computer and video games that seem obscure or even counterintuitive at first.[35] One such development, which can often appear mystifying from the outside, is the procedural creation of digital (and, to a lesser degree, analogue) game worlds. This approach is currently associated primarily with games like *No Man's Sky* (2016) and *Dwarf Fortress* (2006–) and often used for economic reasons, as it saves time otherwise spent on manually designing expansive in-game environments. However, as early as the 1980s, game designers like David Braben and Chris Crawford explored the then-new generative capacities of computers and consoles like the Atari VCS, such as by creating maps from "polygonal regions" (Crawford 2003, 346) or realistic-sounding names via "letter-pair frequency table[s]" (347). As posited in the introduction to this book based on Lev Manovich's analysis of Photoshop (Manovich 2013), design tools shape the creator's view of the spectrum of possible outcomes of a design process. For instance, *Celeste* (2018) lead designer Matt Thorson detailed his diagrammatic process of planning levels in a 2017 GDC session, which led him to understand the one-screen levels that constitute the larger world of *Celeste* as self-contained "stories"; the visual abstraction enabled him to adopt a macrostructural view on the game's progression as an "emerging narrative" (Jenkins 2007).[36] World-making tools like *Articy Draft* frame a game world as a network of different document types such as maps, genealogies, biographies, and segments of backstory, which writers can collaboratively edit.[37] By including more and more functions to connect these documents, the procedural rhetoric of *Articy Draft* incentivizes making the network increasingly dense and frames that density as a benchmark for creating realistic virtual worlds.

Worldbuilding in games has long been used to "enchant" the technological limitations of software tools by translating them into a narrative whole, a process often called *semanticization.* For instance, Murray (1997) pointed out how the text adventure game *Zork* (1980) provided a fantastical context for the "object-oriented software design" of LISP, "which made it particularly easy to define new objects and categories of objects" (78).

The same applies to the controversial *No Man's Sky*, which pioneered the procedural creation of entire planets and biomes but was accused of being an empty virtual world rather than an actual game. In interviews and announcements, lead designer Sean Murray's rhetoric illustrates how building procedural content creation (PCC) tools can develop a momentum of its own. For instance, Murray stated, somewhat reluctantly, that "whilst the game idea did come first and the tech second, [the developers] are sort of a little bit in love with it."[38]

Demoing the tool to a game journalist, Murray constantly moves the in-game camera while talking, formulating and testing hypotheses about what a particular section of environment might look like and simultaneously reveling in the epistemic stability of his virtual world. He emphasizes the fact that "you don't have to actually store any information about it,"[39] which adds plausibility to the metaphor of creation, as it focuses on the creative "intent" of the black-boxed PCC algorithms rather than man-made data objects. Similarly, using Facebook's news feed algorithm as an example, Bogost (2016) argues that due to "the elegant simplicity of [the] algorithms" and their constant black-boxed tweaking, we are "elevating those services [like Facebook or Google] to the divine rank of gods."

Despite its ongoing popularity, PCC will not be the only new paradigm for virtual worlds. Actually, partly in opposition to its inflationary use in recent years, the notion of "handcrafted" worlds or overall aesthetics has increasingly permeated discussions about digital games.[40] From a tool perspective, it is important to acknowledge that highly complex PCC tools used for big budget games like *No Man's Sky* coexist with numerous, partially redundant variations of simpler PCC algorithms in small independent games. For instance, the source files for *Spelunky* (2018), an early iconic PCC title, were made available online in 2013, enabling aspiring designers to copy, modify, and recirculate its PCC routines.[41] This bifurcated development, and the increasing mainstream awareness of PCC principles it fosters, gradually alters the collective imaginary of what a (digital) game world—and game authorship for that matter—is or at least can be.

Defaults, Templates, and Archetypes in Character Customization Tools

As suggested earlier, tools often unnoticeably but tangibly shape our understanding of the material we process when using them. Similar discussions have emerged in the digital humanities, where tool use is increasingly scrutinized because it shapes how scholars interpret cultural data and corresponding social issues.

For instance, Rieder and Röhle (2012) differentiate between *auxiliary* and *heuristic tools*; while the former "target 'auxiliary' functions such as communication, knowledge organization, archiving, or pedagogy," the latter are "constitutive for the discovery or production of new knowledge" (69). Heuristic tools shape our view on the material at hand "by rendering certain aspects, properties, or relations visible" (70), and the power of default interface options, templates, and archetypes plays a central role in that process. The same also applies to game creation, especially if the material reflects norms and values discussed in a broader social context, as in the case of in-game character customization tools. Character editors have been a part of role-playing and sports games particularly for years; for instance, the Gold Box engine, designed to create role-playing games like *Pools of Radiance* (1988), prominently featured character customization. Currently, these systems are highly relevant to many; for instance, Steam specifically allows for browsing and searching for games that include character customization.[42]

Most basically, these tools require breaking up the visual representation of the character into separately modifiable segments like the head, torso, or apparel.[43] The "procedural rhetoric" here lies primarily in the interface. Interface elements like social functionality, menu options, or the page layout of a website are "both reflecting and reinforcing social logics" (Stanfill 2015). Accordingly, menus especially fulfill a rhetorical purpose by including and excluding, as well as ordering, a contingent set of options. In addition, default settings inevitably communicate underlying norms and values, regardless of how intentional their design has been. McArthur, Teather, and Jenson (2015) have compared character customization features in a matrix, which shows that, with a few exceptions like *Jam City Rollergirls* (2011) or *Saints*

Row 2 (2008), Caucasian male templates are common default settings. The authors also point out unique design choices, such as the body shape slider (237) in *Saints Row 2*, which enables players to select a proportion of male and female body characteristics on a scale from -50 to 50, attributing female characteristics to negative and male to positive numbers.

More recently, the online role-playing game *Black Desert Online* (2014–) introduced one of the most intensely debated character customization tools to date. Developed by Korean studio Pearl Abyss, the default characters clearly reflect the unusually formalized beauty standards in South Korea, which include to "be thin, as pale as possible, have big eyes, double eyelids and a very delicate jaw" (Vdovychenko and Lupu 2018). These criteria, which combine the exaggerated aesthetics of anime characters with "the normalization of homogeneous, 'westernized' beauty," are fueled by social media practices like selfies, as well

Figure 2.5
Character customization in Black Desert Online (https://www.youtube.com/watch?v=KKSRpOrR6xQ).

as beautification apps like Cymera. In that context, *Black Desert* both reflects existing cultural sentiments and simultaneously shapes them, by making the self appear easily malleable, a set of parameters that can be tweaked at will.

The few existing studies on character customization focus on features of tools rather than content produced with them and thus do not acknowledge the increasingly critical and subversive uses players have found for them. While earlier games only allowed for selecting predefined characters, games like *Black Desert* parametrize many aspects of a character's face and body, which notably increases the player's agency. For instance, players started to host competitions to create the most unattractive *Black Desert* character possible, usually by exploring extreme combinations of parameters.[44] While these competitions seek to expose and potentially resist the normative beauty standards in the tool's procedural rhetoric, other players attempt to recreate famous fictional characters to develop and playfully perform their own (popular) media literacy. A representative Imgur gallery of *Dragon's Dogma* (2012) content includes several recreations of fictional characters, but also politicians like Hillary Clinton and Donald Trump, who thus also are interpreted in similar categories, as character archetypes.[45] As an auxiliary tool (to adapt the distinction by Rieder and Röhle), Imgur allows for sharing the parameters used to create the characters as numerical values next to the screenshots. This affords re-creation and, as a consequence, incentivizes other players to try out and experiment with these settings. Thus, combined with image-sharing platforms, character customization tools can also afford playful learning, as players can retrace their steps, formulate minihypotheses, and—by testing them—discover new hypotheses.[46] They inspire competition, as players can imitate and then try to refine the original designs, using platforms like Imgur or the games' own forums to compare the results with a like-minded community.[47] Thus, the same software applications that are often (deliberately or not) designed to reify and thus perpetuate narrow representations of gender, ethnicity, and perceived beauty can simultaneously become tools for experimenting with new aesthetics of the self by visually exploring new archetypes, if players maintain a critical and playful disposition towards them.

Finally, the power of defaults is not limited to character creation tools; in fact, the "hypercasual" game creation tool Buildbox mentioned at the beginning of this chapter offers *templates*, ready-made game archetypes that players can modify. These templates include, for example, 360 Shooter, a template called Around the World for 2-D games with planetoid physics like *SLI-FI*, and a vertical avoidance game.[48] The templates contribute

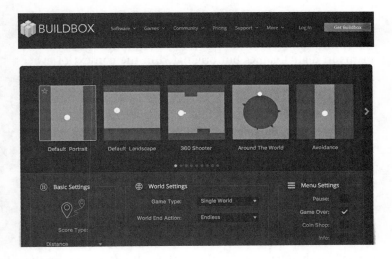

Figure 2.6
Buildbox templates. Screenshot of the official Buildbox website (https://web.archive.org/web/20180720135633/https://www.buildbox.com/buildbox/).

to the omnipresence of game clones for mobile devices and, in the eyes of a Buildbox user, discursively frame this situation as "natural." Due to the amount of games created every month, new game genres increasingly bubble up as microgenres from popular discourse, often through association with iconic games like *QWOP* (2008), a "comedic video game" (Jones 2016) that inspired a microgenre eventually "dubbed 'fumblecore'" (86). This particularly applies to games for mobile platforms, where imitation of successful concepts—and thus also the emergence of corresponding microgenres—occurs at a more rapid pace, and the use of defaults and templates in mobile game engines like Buildbox both reflects and fosters that cultural logic.[49]

Workflows as Self-Imposed Feedback Loops

Positive and negative feedback loops are systems of control that, according to Salen and Zimmerman (2004), are common elements in digital games but originated in the context of cybernetics in the late 1940s, and thus "precede the advent of digital computers" (214).

They take in user input, feed it back to the user, and provide context that enables users to assess their performance and requires them to adapt their input accordingly. Goetz (2011) illustrates the principle using the example of dynamic speed displays, "a speed limit posting coupled with a radar sensor attached to a huge digital readout announcing 'Your Speed.'" He critiques the feedback loop as the product of an overly technocentric Cold War mindset, but also shows how, in different guises, it only now increasingly manifests itself in everyday life.

A game development example that exemplifies the traditional use of feedback loops comes from Shenja van der Graaf's ethnographic work at Valve and Linden Labs in the form of the Love Machine (486). According to this evocatively labeled system, "Lindens [employees at Linden Labs] give and receive 'love' from their colleagues such as getting help writing code, which at the end of each quarter, results in a pink envelope with money in it, as every 'love note' received translates into US$ 1." Translating love into a quasicurrency that can be accumulated and compared is very much in line with the logic of video games, and because the scores are published on an internal wiki, they make giving and receiving help visible and usable as feedback, similar to the speed meter in Goetz's explanation of feedback loops. More importantly, though, Goetz argues that we started to characteristically impose feedback loops on ourselves, both in everyday practice (e.g., working out with a Fitbit wristband) and in professional contexts like game design. Specific workflows such as maintaining a development log can fulfill such a function. For instance, Willy Chyr, who kept an excessively detailed log of his game *Manifold Garden* (2019), argues: "The devlog helps me remember what I did, why I did it, what worked, and what didn't."[50] Its inherently linear structure, like a chronicle ordering texts as events in time, enabled the devlog to both serve as a way for Chyr to communicate with himself through feedback loops and to simultaneously act as a repository. In that sense, it is similar to a story bible used in collaborative media production contexts (Parkin 2009), only in this case written to mediate between Chyr himself as the only designer and his audience. In his 2014 GDC presentation, Matthew Durby advocated using comics to document game design processes for a similar reason.[51] Re-presenting earlier choices in a different format, such as seeing game production decisions through the lens of a comic strip character, can start a feedback loop that enables developers to rethink and adapt subsequent decisions accordingly.

When discussing these workflows as self-imposed feedback loops, it is important to acknowledge that the notion of *work-flow* suggests a continuous, natural, quintessentially "human" process, which is often associated with traditional craftsmanship. Yet tools have always broken processes down into discrete chunks. For instance, media scholar Marshall McLuhan (1994), still differentiating between tools as "extend[ing] the fist, the nails, the teeth, the arm" and machines as a more complex "extension or outering of a process," refers to printing as the "first complete mechanization of a handicraft" that "breaks up the movement of the hand into a series of discrete steps" (152). A similar transformation applies to game development, which shifted from the more continuous writing of assembler code (see, e.g., Montfort and Bogost 2009) into discrete steps, producing and manipulating an assemblage of code, media objects, and data, which is both required for and further propagated by self-imposing feedback loops. Finally, because feedback loops are closely related to the notion of *core loops* in game and gamification design, companies can use games to leverage them as an indirect, decentralized form of control over external development processes.[52] For instance, Google and other technology platforms have been producing and sharing small games for new hardware projects like Google Glass.[53]

As sample projects (see the tool essay on amateur and professional creator identities earlier in this chapter for details on sample projects as rhetorical affordances), these games can become tools that inspire developer engagement. Aspiring developers use the games as input for their first design experiments, producing and sharing variations on the given theme, which then become

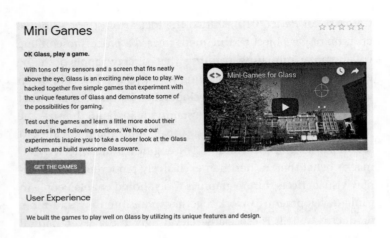

Figure 2.7
Google Glass minigames.

context for new iterations of the feedback loop. However, while predefining a ludic approach toward a new technology seems to frame it as something to play with, it can simultaneously prevent truly "appropriative" (Sicart 2014, 11) and potentially even "disruptive" (14) forms of play.

Tools Becoming More "Human"

In handbooks suggesting best practices for tool-making and tool use, the human user is often "designed" as an accessory, a product of the software. This is implied, for example, in the use of "personas as a practical tool for design," the formulation of a fictional character that "depicts an ideal user" (Chen and Liu 2015). However, over the past ten years of game technology, this relationship appears to have been gradually subverted. For instance, the MegaTexture technology, developed by John

Carmack for *Rage* (2010), shifted the focus from the traditional creation of per-object texture maps toward a process resembling collaborative miniature painting that directly applied to the entire game world, thus affording novel relationships between artists and coders during development. Carmack stated that "we've got this whole team, our 'stamp squad' [and] they use the MegaTexture tools, where they just fly around and they can start sort of painting in the world."[54] The engine feature reflected Carmack's belief that, rather than exclusively rendering more complex visual effects, future graphics tools should enable people in game development to work together more intensely and more productively. This is especially relevant given that even natural practices like writing for games are directly dependent on the tool context. Leigh Alexander, writer for the Unity-based *Reigns: Her Majesty* (2017), argues that "before you have a grasp on the tools, you don't really know how you're going to express yourself through words."[55]

As game design becomes an increasingly widespread cultural practice and "playing and building" become more akin to "reading and writing" (Caperton 2012, 1), a development that according to Caperton fosters "game-media literacy" (8), it becomes more common for creators to express themselves by creating highly idiosyncratic tools. For instance, a Reddit user called fek_ created an online tool to make it easier for Dungeons & Dragons game masters to handle jumping in the game.[56] These personal systems of organization can sometimes "trickle up" into professional contexts. Members of the *Team Fortress 2* community started creating demo levels containing all 3-D assets of a specific type or theme, grouped by category. These levels were colloquially called a *zoo*, and they prefigure the level designer's imagination differently than previously used text-based asset

lists—for instance, by enabling new forms of visual association.[57] Valve later adopted the same system to create levels for
Counter Strike: Go (2012). Even more evocatively, an anonymous
graphics programmer at Epic Games created a "squint tool" in
Unreal Engine 3.[58] He or she allegedly watched artists squint-
ing repeatedly to switch between close-up looks and taking in
the overall composition of an image and then wrote a script to
reenact that habit with a click of a button by blurring the frame
buffer. In these cases, making tools is so quick that it can be part
of a larger process rather than necessarily a separate project as
was the case before.

Finally, as tools become more "human," it is important to also
acknowledge the opposite—that is, essentially human practices
being perceived and redesigned as tools. This can be observed
in Scrum, a widely used, tried, and tested project management
framework that has been increasingly adopted in the digital
game industry (Keith 2010). In Scrum, team meetings (referred
to as *daily scrums*) are formalized to the point that they are perceived as tools rather than forms of social interaction between
human beings. They are strictly time-boxed, such as being limited to fifteen minutes; ideally held in the same location and at
the same time of day; are guided by well-defined questions; and
usually take place with all participants standing up. All these
characteristics can be understood as sociotechnical affordances;
that is, they serve to defamiliarize the meeting as a social gath-
ering, and by following these guidelines, participants perform as
parts of an almost algorithmically structured system.

Even more recently, the ambiguity—and also limitations—of
conceptualizing people as tools can be seen in the use of real-
life actors in game creation, including but not limited to performance capture. For example, Quantic Dream, a game studio

famous for ambitious interactive movies like *Detroit: Become Human* (2018), combined data from multiple real-life actors in its earlier games. Lucas Kane, the protagonist of *Fahrenheit* (2005), comprises traces of eight different actors, including body language, stunt animations, facial expressions (through a puppeteer), and voice (Cage 2006). The relationship between actors and digital production has become increasingly dialogical and iterative. For instance, for *Beyond: Two Souls* (2013), Quantic Dream developers wondered why the virtual renditions of the characters at first did not create the desired level of recognizability. By making incremental changes to the character design and offsetting their effects against the lived experience with Ellen Page, who plays Jodie Holmes in the game, the hairstyle was ultimately identified as the main epistemic gap between the game character and the real-life actress.[59] Another related example is the street scene in *Beyond: Two Souls*, in which players can make Jodie play the guitar and sing along. Thomsen (2013) reports that "the scene as originally planned by [David] Cage had no option for players to try and sing" but that the designer "noticed Page playing a guitar he'd brought to the studio and decided to record her." Allegedly, "Cage was so moved by her voice and performance that he decided to write it in as one of the choices players could make for the sequence." An interview with Neil Druckmann, director of *The Last of Us* (2013), similarly hints at the agency that actors can have despite being tools in a standardized production process. Druckmann elaborates on how the unique sense of humor of voice actress Ashley Johnson directly informed the writing of the character Ellie in the game, adding a unique and originally not intended angle to the otherwise rather depressing or at least melancholic dystopian game scenario.[60] As suggested earlier, the presence and performance of actors is never completely reduced to digital data, such as reusable animation data in sharable file formats. This raises important questions about the agency of more traditional tools as well. For instance, cultural scholar and academic filmmaker Mieke Bal (2013) argues that images should be regarded as tools (or as "theoretical objects"; 52) in humanities research contexts because they can "speak back, resist (parts of) my interpretation of them, and make me think" (52). In chapter 3 of this book, we will address in more detail this question of how evocative and (occasionally) resistive tools can and should be.

Acknowledging Tool Evolution

One key difference between digital and (most) physical tools is that they can and, by now, usually do evolve and profoundly change over time. From that angle, existing analyses of software affordances like Lev Manovich's aforementioned work on Adobe Photoshop, Claus Pias and Wolfgang Coy's investigation of how PowerPoint changes the way we think visually (Pias and Coy 2009), or Matthew Curinga's critical analysis of software affordances (Curinga 2014) are not fully equipped to investigate digital tools because they usually only interpret the functionality of a tool at the time of writing. Taking the Steam distribution platform as an example, Werning (2019) argues that the procedural rhetoric of a tool is as much defined by the choreography of feature changes over time as by the interplay of features and design affordances at a given point in time. The same argument is rather obvious if applied to digital games per se; for players of highly mutable massive multiplayer games like *Fortnite* (2017–) or *Destiny* (2014–), it often matters more which affordances are added or taken away than which are implemented at any particular moment, not least because players interpret these games in a much broader temporal context than earlier "immutable" game distributed on disk or CD-ROM. GameMaker is but one game-making tool that has undergone major changes since its launch as an educational side project in 1999.[61] The most basic affordance change already lies in the name. By departing from the numbered iterations of GameMaker that ended with version 8.0 and adding the Studio label , developer YoYo Games signified a cut, breaking with the past and opening up a new chapter in the history of the tool. One way to map these affordance changes in GameMaker: Studio involves comparing the accompanying release notes.[62] For instance, the tool rhetorically positions itself through the ongoing inclusion of but lack of updates for its built-in 3-D functionality, which was introduced in 2004 with version 6.0. Because the—comparatively rudimentary—3-D functions are still implemented but have not been notably improved upon in recent updates, they serve as a persistent reminder of 3-D as a development trajectory that is clearly framed as part of the tool's past but not its future. More recently, Chief Technology Officer (CTO) Russell Kay explained changes planned for the second half of 2019, and most feature additions like chained accessors, method variables, or exception support do not provide novel opportunities for novice creators but instead make Game-Maker's GML language more familiar to users of general-purpose programming languages like C++ or C#, thus repositioning the tool as suitable for professional development work.[63] In some cases, affordance changes even rhetorically contribute to a company's tool vision, as with the alleged "death of Flash" (Salter and Murray 2014, 3) and its ongoing legacy within the game industry. Responding to Steve Jobs's rejection of Flash on iOS devices in 2010, Adobe stopped further development of Flash plug-ins on mobile devices, but also visibly invested in HTML5 development tools and even created a JavaScript library to help Flash users transition to HTML5. Apart from their functional value for Flash users, all these decisions were aimed at rhetorically positioning Adobe as proactive, taking a self-determined stance rather than reacting to Apple's "attack."

Whereas the previous section primarily argued why considering tools from a diachronic perspective is important and how the rhetoric of feature changes can be conceptualized, the last chapter of the book next will offer suggestions for how game creation tools should evolve and will explain why their evolution is directly tied to the evolution of games as an expressive medium in itself.

3 A Call for Evocative Tool Design: Game Creation as . . .

One recurring theme in all the tool essays in chapter 2 is the increasing intermingling of game creation and tool creation, which exhibit several commonalities in terms of design (procedural rhetoric) and interaction (playful use). Yet discussions among video game fans and even journalists still often operate with diffuse definitions of game creation tools—as evidenced, for example, by a controversy surrounding the launch of *Fallout 76* (2018) and developer Bethesda Softworks's strategy concerning the future development of its in-house game engine. A quote from creative director Todd Howard about why the developers have come to "like [their] editor" was taken out of context and critiqued as an alleged confirmation that Bethesda planned to keep the same engine for its upcoming games.[1] Even though Howard also points, in the same quote, to multiple components that were changed already for *Fallout 76*, like "a new renderer, a new lighting system and a new system for the landscape generation," the modular nature of a game engine appears difficult to unpack. This points to several interrelated underlying questions: What exactly is the tool here? How can a tool comprise multiple smaller tools in sometimes varying configurations? And how do tools shape our understanding of game-making as a cultural practice? Successful game design—such as the mystifying complexity hidden in the simple ruleset of a game like Go—is still often perceived as "magic" rather than craft. In her 2018 GDC session, game design Jennifer Scheurle documents several hidden design techniques that have been honed "for decades" to make compelling gameplay appear "like a magic trick."[2] While some players cherish this perception—like a museum visitor not wanting to know too much about an artwork so as to not diminish its aura—there is value in striving for more clarity on how (game) tools work. Only then can we go beyond simply improving tools and begin making tool design—like good game design—more evocative.

Currently, the few explicit calls for tool design within the game industry focus on optimization. For example, in his 2016 GDC presentation, Robin-Yann Storm reports on his comparison of level editor designs, characteristically formulating the goal of these editors as "keeping level designers in the zone."[3] The term "in the zone" clearly—albeit not explicitly—alludes to the notion of flow in games (Chen 2007)—that is, trying to keep players in a psychologically rewarding state, in which competencies and challenges increase in synchronicity. In other words, Storm is looking for a particular—intuitively relatable—form of procedural rhetoric in the tools, though it is only one among many potentially viable design strategies. Other goals formulated by Storm, such as to "speed up the process of level design iteration" or to "make levels more complex" (Chen 2007), are characteristically quantitative and suggest a focus on incremental improvements. A design research comparison of analogue and digital graphics design tools (Stones and Cassidy 2007) exhibits a similarly quantitative approach, aiming to determine which tools work "best" in which use case.

However, just like evocative games should not keep players "in the zone" at all times but should also temporarily puzzle or even irritate them in order to challenge their preconceptions, tool design can and eventually should do more than that as well. For that purpose, it is important to briefly concretize the term *evocative*. Sherry Turkle (2007) uses the term *evocative objects* to describe how things contain traces of the people that own and use them. Even more, the term emphasizes the "inseparability of thought and feeling in our relationship to things" because "we think with the objects we love [and] we love the objects we think with" (5). Any avid user of a particular tool, be it physical or digital, will likely recognize these aspects, both of which go beyond mere questions of convenience or productivity. The concept has been tentatively explored in design contexts, usually with the goal of embedding it into a particular method. For instance, Su and Liang (2013) suggest that designers should bring their own "evocative objects" into a project to "enrich . . . the quality of experiential interaction design" (610), but do not acknowledge tools as evocative objects in themselves. Turkle's use of the term *evocative* points to the idiosyncratic or, more generally, distinctly human aspects of tools-as-objects. Matthew Curinga expresses a similar sentiment in his critical perspective on software affordances, arguing that "tools and technology are inextricably human" and that "technology [including the use of software tools] is one of the fundamental expressions of human cultural activity" (Curinga 2014).

A perspective on evocative tool design not only raises the question of what (video) game creation actually is, but can also challenge us to think about what it could be. In 2003, Espen Aarseth argued that play itself should be regarded as a method (Aarseth 2003, 3–4) within game studies as a discipline because the experience of play cannot easily be substituted by, say, watching others play or reading a game manual. Following the analogy of games and tools as a "red thread" through this book, the same can be said about the experience of game creation, which is also almost impossible to replicate by other means and has to be experienced to be fully understood. In many arguments, the essence of game creation is, for practical reasons, often defined based on the author's own interests and background. For example, based on his extensive ethnographic field work, Casey O'Donnell frames video game development primarily as a "creative collaborative practice" (O'Donnell 2009). The argument focuses on the people involved in the process, and thus characteristically frames game creation as part of the developers' "everyday lives," shaped by, for example, "tensions between work and play." By distilling common themes from the tool essays in chapter 2, this concluding chapter aims to formulate five alternative ways to (re)frame tool use, particularly but not exclusively in game creation contexts, as a playful, performative, narrative, analytical, and communicative process. Each of these framings helps shed light on aspects that otherwise often remain unnoticed or are easily taken for granted. These five categories are not mutually exclusive; on the contrary, they usually manifest themselves in particular combinations and can often be traced back to specific aspects of a tool's procedural rhetoric. Consider an example from music production: digital audio workstation Reason, originally created in 2001, is famous for a feature called Toggle Rack, which allows users to turn their virtual devices around and manually reroute the virtual but physically modeled audio cables that connect them.

This notable departure from earlier interface conventions, which is likely not the most efficient but certainly an evocative

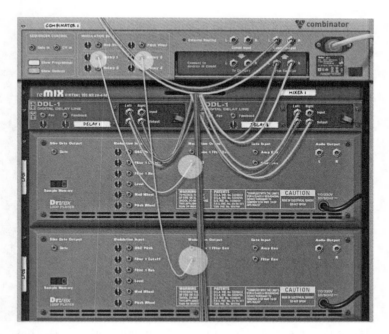

Figure 3.1
Screenshot of Reason's Toggle Rack functionality (https://www.reason-experts.com/the-hydlide-guide-of-the-combinator-part-one.html).

design choice, illustrates a combination of at least three of the five characteristics: playfulness, communication, and performativity. First, the physics simulation affords object play (Riede et al. 2018): it incentivizes both novice and expert users, depending on their playful disposition, to experiment with the simulated physical behavior of the cables and to appreciate the visual constellations created by re-reconnecting virtual sequencers and drum machines. Second, it affords interesting ways of communicating with an audience, such as via tutorial videos or videos made to share one's own virtual setups. Finally, the feature enables a particular form of identity performance. For novice users, it allows for reenacting practices considered iconic of professional audio production. For experts, it allows for emulating familiar ways of working with physical audio equipment that they might not have used for some time, thereby reaffirming their relationship with the material quality of their tools and rediscovering the impact of the tools on their own identity as audio producers.

. . . a Playful Process

As the book departs from the central assumption that procedural rhetoric can also be applied to design tools, it appears plausible to consider the game creation process as game-like in itself. O'Donnell (2014) intuitively "conceptualiz[es] the videogame industry as a game" (252). In this context, the game is primarily a metaphor, as O'Donnell considers his ethnography "a design document or videogame development work" (252). That development work allegedly "functions as the core gameplay mechanics," "stylized in the form of puzzle-like tasks that the player navigates" (262), and O'Donnell creatively maps common practices in game development to "game subsystems" like skill levels (263).

Ahead, these arguments are unpacked further and placed in a broader theoretical context by focusing on the implications of tool-making and tool use. From an evolutionary point of view, both tool use and tool-making appear inextricably linked to play. For instance, Riede et al. (2018) discuss archeological evidence of *object play*, which arguably enabled man to develop from "us[ing] simple tools and perform[ing] simple activities through autonomous exploratory play" to creating "complex tools such as the bow and arrow . . . often manufactured by specialists" (47). According to that argument, "the active provisioning of children with play objects—sometimes functional miniatures of adult tools—and the encouragement of object play" (46) have been vital for mankind to develop tools and foster innovation. For instance, some of the earliest examples of wheels have been found in "small zoomorphic ceramic vessels" that "may be interpreted as ritual paraphernalia . . . or, indeed, as children's play objects" (51).

Applying this perspective to game creation, though, raises a few questions. For game developers seeking to earn a living, the stakes are unmistakably very high, which might make it difficult to imagine the development process in terms of play. Indeed, it would not, for example, conform to Johan Huizinga's canonical but also narrow definition of play as a voluntary activity that is an end in itself rather than practiced, say, for monetary gains. However, the tension and precariousness but also the exhilaration, such as after a physically demanding phase of crunch time, that characterizes professional game design can be usefully understood as *deep play* (Geertz 1972). Ethnographer Clifford Geertz applied the concept to cock fighting on Bali, which was enjoyed by many as a clandestine cultural practice despite being officially illegal. Knowing about the dangers adds to the social meaning of deep play activities. In fact, Geertz reports being welcomed into the play community after attending a cock fight broken up by the authorities and subsequently hiding from the police with fellow players. Engaging in game-making despite the tangible risks is similarly seen as a rite of passage into a play community. For example, Guevara-Villalobos (2011) points to how "informational networking" (6) or sharing work samples and expert knowledge as "a practice of 'opening up'" (8) produces a sense of "camaraderie" (7) in the independent game community. According to Villalobos's ethnographic insights, independent game creators arguably "develop trustful bonds [and] reinforce common values, goals and practices" (11), similar to people playing games together over a longer period of time.

To exemplify how tool use is making game creation more playful, Bernard Suits's previously introduced definition of games as systems of artificial constraints (see the section "A Production Studies Perspective on Digital Games" in chapter 1) can be traced back to several recent tools that have built a cult following, especially among amateur developers. For instance, the open-source HTML5 puzzle game engine PuzzleScript challenges developers to fit their game concepts into a very limited set of

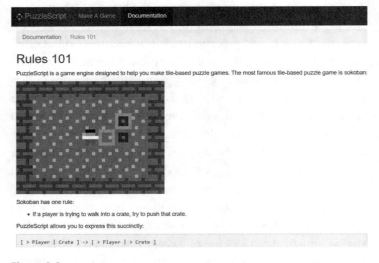

Figure 3.2
Screenshot of the PuzzleScript website (https://www.puzzlescript.net/Documentation/rules101.html).

movement and push mechanics, reminiscent of, for example, the puzzle game *Sokoban* (1982).[4]

Characteristically, just like avid players begin to interpret the world through the lens of their games, aspiring developers started reimagining familiar game concepts within the scope of PuzzleScript. For instance, games like *Funky Bird* reference the iconic mobile game *Flappy Bird* (2013), while *Overrwyrld* goes back to the original *The Legend of Zelda* (1986).[5] The choice of source material suggests that the developers interpret this as a self-imposed challenge, a type of game Caillois and Halperin (1955) call *agon* (65), not least because the original games both function very differently from the regular PuzzleScript mechanics and had to be significantly redesigned to fit the limitations of the tool. The same applies to games like *Flying Kick*, which pursues the ambitious aim to translate fighting game mechanics that normally require precise physics simulation and timing into the turn-based framework of PuzzleScript.[6] Players often aim to explore the boundaries of game mechanics, either with a playfully transgressive mindset or to identify and exploit quirks in their game's behavior that can help them improve their performance, such as in games like the *Mario Kart* franchise (Bainbridge and Bainbridge 2007, 65–67). PuzzleScript affords a similar game-like approach, and the popularity of the aforementioned games suggests that—within the PuzzleScript community—this playful approach is valorized. Indeed, even though PuzzleScript is almost a tool-game hybrid, it has occasionally been used by independent designers, such as for level design prototyping in larger puzzle games like *A Good Snowman Is Hard to Build* (2017) that look different but utilize similar mechanics.[7] The same pattern can be found in other tools like the (even more minimalistic) Flickgame, which is used to create graphic adventure games controlled exclusively by clicking on specific colors in images.[8] The play experience of these highly constrained tools is similar to that described in discussions of games, such as about choosing the similarly constrained Deprived character class in *Dark Souls* (2011). Both PuzzleScript and *Dark Souls* (specifically the Deprived class) require and reward bricolage (see the tool essay on bricolage in chapter 2), which Louridas (1999) describes as inherently playful since the bricoleur's "universe of tools is closed, and the rule of his game is to always make do with 'what's available,' that is, a set, finite at each instance, of tools and materials." In both cases, the obvious limitations are experienced both as liberating and as an opportunity to learn how to "play well," which can make the process itself "the most rewarding, helps you learn, and makes for a better story."[9]

Apart from actual software tools, game jams, especially considering how they are deployed by professional companies like Double Fine or Blizzard, also should be regarded as a semiformalized tool, facilitating a playful approach toward game creation. They provide rules of play that afford serendipitous discovery in a controlled environment and, as in most games, the more evocative rules like the "diversifiers" of the Global Game Jam usually stimulate more inspired and experimental playing strategies.[10] Several commercial games like Double Fine's *Hack'N'Slash* (2014) and *Space Base DF9* (2014) were originally prototyped during in-house game jams, which specifically allowed for an audience of early adopters to form around these projects, helped the developer gauge interest, and informed the ongoing development. Blizzard regularly organizes game jams to let its developers play with its flagship title *Diablo III* (2012).[11] In that context, the actual game becomes both tool and playing field for playful cocreation—which, for instance, resulted in the inclusion of the Necromancer class in *Diablo III*. Creating the class was not only a design challenge—as *Diablo III* plays differently than its predecessor, which made the Necromancer popular; the design also required rhetorical finesse because the character class was a fan favorite and could have easily been "misinterpreted" in the eyes of both staff and fans using a more traditional, top-down decision-making process.

As playful competitions, game jams can be categorized using Caillois's taxonomy (Caillois and Halperin 1955), which most basically distinguishes among games of competition (*agon*), luck or fate (*alea*), role-play and simulation (*mimicry*), and immersion or flow (*vertigo*). Agon in game jams is stimulated by competitive mechanics, such as the different grading criteria like innovation, mood, and humor in jams like Ludum Dare or the aforementioned diversifiers, which, like achievements, allow for accumulating "gaming capital" (Sotamaa 2009).[12] Aspects of alea come from random themes (which are only communicated on short notice), as well as, if applicable, the team composition, because single participants are often expected to find and work with different collaborators. Mimicry can be found in acting out the role of the game designer—a persona that is often marginalized in everyday social interaction—and by imitating and appropriating what others are doing (or simply borrowing from influential commercial games). Finally, the sense of urgency imposed by the time limit, as well as the physical and mental exhaustion that comes from working on a game jam project with few interruptions for forty-eight hours or more, creates a sense of vertigo, an experience that Caillois originally attributes to game-like activities like whirling dances or extreme sports.

Finally, understanding game design as a playful process, it makes sense to contextualize the work of game studios and developers in terms of player typologies. For instance, Tuunanen and Hamari (2012) compared different player categories based on geographic, demographic, psychographic and behavioral characteristics (2–3), but given the scope of this argument, it will suffice to focus here on the "four archetypes" (6). Richard Bartle, cocreator of *MUD1* and one of the pioneers of the massively multiplayer online game (MMO) industry, specified these four player types to describe common dispositions toward games. For instance, the so-called achievers aim to attain and demonstrate mastery over every aspect of a game, while the socializers primarily consider games as vehicles for social interactions with others. Framing creators as players has already been productively applied to filmmakers. For instance, Simons (2007) convincingly investigated the work of Lars von Trier and his collaborators through the lens of games. For the documentary *The Five Obstructions* (2002), von Trier "has the director Jørgen Leth make five variations of his earlier short film *The Perfect Human. . .* , each with increasingly sadistic commands and difficult-to-overcome limitations" (23–24). This approach can be useful, for example, to contextualize the development of unique games like *Unearthed: Trail of Ibn Battuta* (2013). Developed by multiplatform development studio Semaphore, based in Riyadh, *Unearthed* is an episodic action-adventure game that combines familiar genre elements with a decidedly non-Western setting and characters. It was criticized for its poor production values, but, as an ambitious project from an emerging game development region like Saudi Arabia, the development of *Unearthed* exhibits important aspects of play behavior. For example, it demonstrates an achiever mentality as one of the first games developed for the PlayStation 3 using Unity. Unlike the killer in Bartle's model, achievers don't primarily aim to surpass others but focus on the game itself—in this case, on mastering the intricacies of console game development and publishing. It also demonstrates an explorer mindset, a player type concerned with experiencing and systematically uncovering everything a game has to offer. In the case of *Unearthed*, this refers to experimenting with episodic storytelling, planning a free-to-play multiplayer component via Facebook, and mapping out and systematically adapting both story and gameplay elements of the *Uncharted* franchise.[13] While especially mimicking the popular *Uncharted* series, considered by many as a benchmark of AAA game development at the time, fueled criticism among gamers, the notion of player types can help bring these unusual development contexts into perspective instead of writing them off as creators failing to meet industry standards.

. . . as a Performative Process

In his 2016 GDC presentation, Rami Ismail, cofounder of Dutch independent game studio Vlambeer, uses the term *performative game design* to characterize the creation of *Nuclear Throne* (2015). The studio decided to livestream development to counter idea theft and piracy—that is, to create an engaged audience around the game early on, before copycat games could beat them to market or preliminary versions could be leaked and distributed online.

Ismail does not develop the notion of performativity further in his talk but provides anecdotal evidence of how livestreaming has changed the creation process of *Nuclear Throne*.[14] In that process, both the recording situation and the digital streaming platform emerge as influential tools rather than simply enabling technologies. For instance, Ismail points out initial irritations caused by low-quality recording equipment and emphasizes that committing to livestreaming requires discipline, which can also include postponing other things to stick to a self-imposed broadcast schedule. Rhetorically, the decision to stream tied the game more immediately to its creators, similar to the relationship between a performance artwork and the artist-as-performer. Practically, after its earlier game *Ridiculous Fishing* had been intensely "cloned," Vlambeer hoped to create a loyal following around its next game by sharing knowledge and actively engaging with fans.[15]

By performing game design, Vlambeer is not just perceived as the maker of *Nuclear Throne* but positions itself as an ideal type of a developer embodying a specific set of values and norms, similar to a persona in a Shakespearian play. On their Twitch profile, the developers claim that "game development has been a nebulous concept for long enough."[16] That rhetoric becomes part of a distinct persona, which also includes prominently mentioning that the developers "dropped out of game design university" to make the games they would love to play themselves. The studio thus frames performative game-making as going against conventional wisdom in the industry. Umberto Eco calls this process *ostension*—that is, "de-realizing a given object in order to make it stand for an entire class" (Eco 1977, 110), like when a stage actor uses a concrete object as prop with symbolic implications. Ismail's intuitive use of the term *performative* here is in line with the more general understanding of "designing as performing" (e.g., Binder et al. 2011, 105) in contemporary theories of design practice. From that angle, design constitutes a performance in that it establishes a "structural relationship between experience and expression," which "has an eventlike and processual character" (108). This definition of performance, derived from

Victor Turner, is characteristically ambiguous and can refer to "the everyday, the ritual, the drama, and liminality" (110)—that is, transitional situations such as rites of passage—and indeed all these aspects can potentially inform the performative design process.

Vlambeer aimed at establishing an ongoing, reciprocal relation with its audience, yet the more common forms of development streaming, like creating time-lapse screencasts during game jams using tools like Screencast-O-Matic or ScreenNinja, focus on establishing a temporary connection, usually tied to a specific event.[17]

Most importantly, due to accelerated playback speed, the screencasts do not primarily improve the viewer's understanding of how to make a game, but they make the process experienceable, almost tangible, in a different way. For instance, rather than understanding what happens in each individual tool, the viewer

Figure 3.3
Time-lapse screencast of the Ludum Dare 21 game Henchmen, Attack! (http://getscreenninja.com/videos/henchmen-attack/).

experiences the frequent switching between tools like Unity, Audacity (to create or convert sounds and music), and Photoshop (to create pixel graphics), as well as the preview window, as a form of choreography. The actual development process might be slow and methodical, or fraught with trial and error, but the screencasts are performative in that they imbue it with a kinetic energy. Like binge-watching a television series at a rapid pace, seeing a game prototype evolve—including inevitable detours if something does not work as planned—unveils a different sense of purpose, becoming a "portal . . . right into the heads of [its] creators" (Choi 2011). Thus, like a performance, screen-casting game creation establishes a primarily affective rather than rational relationship between developer and viewer. This relationship is also, for instance, shaped by small personal episodes, such as witnessing the developer watching YouTube (see the video referenced in figure 3.3 at 4'26") or playing music to unwind for a few seconds. These moments are intuitively relatable and thus give the audience a fleeting impression of how aspiring developers integrate game-making into their everyday routines.

As they perform for an audience, screen-casting developers are arguably in a similar position as musicians improvising on a musical theme. In fact, designer Erik Loyer explicitly compares game-making to playing a musical instrument (Loyer 2010). Drawing from jazz history, he emphasizes the embodied experience of playing a musical instrument, which also applies to screen casts. Characteristically, though, Loyer does not explicitly address the role of tools at all. He argues that it is "hard to get away from that feeling of binary-logical specificity" (190–191) that comes with game input; apart from analogue sticks for movement and camera control, most controller inputs are either on or off. Thus, Loyer uses musical comparisons as a conceptual tool to think beyond binaries, describing how he "hooked up the idea of advancing syllable by syllable [in his game] to the recording of [jazz singer Kurt] Elling, with a dynamic display of the lyrics swinging and shaking per your gestures with the Wii-mote as the song plays" (192). Like musicians and their instruments, developers identify with the tools they use, and the constant work with them constitutes an ongoing identity performance. For example, Quantic Dream founder David Cage usually co-opts the persona of the filmmaker in how he frames his approach toward game creation and uses tools as props for performing it. For *Fahrenheit*, Quantic Dream developed an in-house system, which Cage characteristically called the Movie Maker Module (Lessard 2009, 200). He explicitly compared its functionality to Adobe's video editing toolkit, Premiere. Thus, playing the role of film writer and director informs Cage's view on tool development, and the tools in turn become part of performing these roles in the context of game development.

In her seminal book on the "transformative power of performance," Erika Fischer-Lichte argued that performance art challenged the established understanding of art as a "fixed, transferable" work (Fischer-Lichte 2008, 75) "independent of its creator" (18). More than offering the audience a theater piece as text, an artistic performance breaks down the barrier between performer and spectator. That is, rather than representing emotions, performances aim to create them in the spectator, "achieving a lasting alteration of their own bodies" that would ideally prompt them to interact or intervene. This also applies to the relationship between game developer and player. For instance, tech journalist Clive Thompson (2002) compared a variety of Adobe Flash games created after September 11, 2001, that addressed the fear of terrorist attacks and the impending global war on terrorism. Flash allowed for creating these games simply and quickly; thus, Thompson interpreted them as a response to contemporary discourse and as "social comment," as a form of communication. However, because the games' rhetoric is rather basic, it might be more to the point to interpret the creation of these games as a performance, triggering an affective, embodied response, such as an outlet for venting anger, coping with frustration and fear, and even as a form of cathartic release rather than a representation. Thus, while the games did not notably change contemporary societal debates—they had limited success as a new communication channel—they did produce a change in the creators' and players' affective economy (Ahmed 2004).

Apart from their core functionality, tools can serve as props for performing the self. For instance, GameMaker: Studio preserved the *skin*—the user interface (UI) look and feel—of GameMaker 8.1 as a template. This is not just an aesthetic detail; choosing that nondefault skin allowed users to perform their identity as GameMaker veterans. Similar concerns applied to the new dark UI skin that had become iconic of professional tools through its earlier introduction in Adobe Photoshop and similar industry-level software applications. Unity even characteristically limited the dark UI scheme to paying users, which sparked controversial forum discussions.[18]

Finally, a culturally comparative perspective can again serve to illustrate the potential of interpreting game creation in performative terms. For example, the Hezbollah-developed first-person shooter game *Special Force 2: Tale of the Truthful Pledge* (2007) casts players as Hezbollah fighters stationed in Southern Lebanon. The game is rather unremarkable in terms of audiovisual or game design but is relevant from a tools perspective because

it was developed using the AAA game engine CryEngine, origi-
nating as an unlicensed mod of *Far Cry* (2004) and later turned
into a standalone game. As a performance, the development process constitutes an act of appropriating and subverting a foreign
technological asset that had earlier been perceived as oppressive
or at least as abetting Western propaganda. That is, with Fischer-
Lichte, it is not just a representation (i.e., a symbolic act) but
aims to actively bring about change, first in the developer-as-
performer and—in a potential second step—in the real world.
Similar patterns of appropriating foreign technologies in order
to extend one's own message and perceptions to new audi-
ences can be traced back to earlier media-historical contexts. For
instance, Cubitt (1999) elaborates on how Indian film pioneer
Dadasaheb Phalke resorted to "foreign" (123) British film technology in order to create both his first film experiments during
the 1910s and his later devotional films on Indian mythologies.
Yet Phalke also "reinvent[ed]" (123) filming practices and took
control over the technologies, even going as far as to perforate
his own film stock. From that angle, his inspirational performative use of filmmaking tools has been, in a way, as influential as
his actual films.

. . . as a Narrative Process

Like all collective cultural practices, game creation produces its
own *mythologies* (Barthes 2006), foundational narratives that
serve to reaffirm the shared norms and values within or the origins and shared histories of its community. Even though these
narratives themselves are often well known, it is important to be
aware of their functions because (1) within the community they
tend to become "natural" and thus virtually unnoticeable and

(2) outside of the community they can be difficult to properly interpret without the necessary context.

Myths often share common themes, such as character archetypes or similar events. With regard to historical accounts, Hayden White (2014) calls the perpetuation of these themes *emplotment* and distinguishes among four narrative logics that have been used to rationalize historical events: "romance, tragedy, comedy, and satire" (7). White uses these modes to characterize the style of eminent historians, but, more importantly for our purposes, they can be adapted to elucidate the role of storytelling in game creation.

For instance, White describes romance, maybe the most common of all four modes, as "a drama of self-identification," a type of narrative in which character traits are exaggerated and conflicts elevated to a "triumph of good over evil, virtue over vice" (8). An important character archetype is the *auteur*, which combines associations with the creator of a literary work and applies them to filmmaking or, more recently, games. Despite the long and contentious history of the term (and its political implications), common definitions include identifiable "themes, style, or technique" (Schepelern 2005, 106), and even though the concept "was coined in the 1950s and 1960s" (103), it is still influential, in different guises, in mainstream discourse. For instance, controversial game director David Cage has claimed the label for himself, arguing that he does not consider the creation of games like *Heavy Rain* (2010) or *Detroit* (2018) as "doing art," but says that he has developed a recognizable, highly idiosyncratic style, similar to that of a literary author: "I put a lot of myself. I'm not talking about me—I'm talking about what I feel, what I think. *Heavy Rain* was really about me becoming a father, and all the fears that go with it" (Nutt 2012). From that angle, the auteur is not just a character but also a blueprint for how (game) creators interpret and readjust their craft. It appears plausible, then, that *Beyond: Two Souls* (2013) was the first game to be presented at the Tribeca Film Festival, including a dedicated trailer that underscored the game's cinematic ambitions.[19] Distribution tools like Kickstarter, while outside the scope of this book (see the final section of this chapter, which briefly addresses distribution tools and why they were not part of the book's overall argument), arguably revitalized the notion of the auteur in games, as the most heavily funded game projects were usually continuations of venerable franchises spearheaded by veteran designers like Brian Fargo (*Wasteland 2*), Yu Suzuki (*Shenmue III*), and Koji Igarashi (*Bloodstained: Ritual of the Night*) with a distinct style and personality. The Kickstarter campaign affordances, such as personalized pitch videos and high-level pledge tiers that allowed backers to meet the game designers, deliberately cultivated that cult of personality to reach a critical mass.

The concept of emplotment shows that these narrative tropes can exert real-world influence. Hayden White investigated how narratives exert control over the interpretation of historical events; with contemporary figures like David Cage, narratives derive that power from being adopted and perpetuated within the game industry. This can have empowering effects, as illustrated, for example, by numerous stories about single developers making games using iconic AAA game engines like Unreal Engine 4. For instance, discussions about Bing Yang's *Lost Soul Aside* (2019) are clearly reminiscent of White's mode of romance because they stylize the tale of mastering the tool as a David versus Goliath scenario. For instance, the top-voted comments on the official YouTube trailer claim that "this man puts multi-billion dollar corporations to shame" and that a "single dude makes a game

that looks better than most large companies," thus framing Bing
Yang in opposition to large game companies, which are perceived
as dispassionate or even cynical in comparison.[20] Yet these narratives do not need to be commonly accepted in order to be discursively productive because they still dictate the talking points
that those who disagree with them aim to refute. For instance,
in a corresponding Reddit discussion, users try to deconstruct
the role of the "heroic figure" that is attributed to Yang by, for
example, focusing on his use of marketplace assets, which makes
his achievement appear more human again. Moreover, the narrative steers discussions about the tool itself, prompting users to
emphasize how "UE is an engine that puts a lot of focus on making games look good" by making graphical effects like "partical
[sic] effects, . . . lighting, . . . material effects, motion blur and
depth of field" accessible without extensive programming.[21]

If game development can be conceived as a metagame, it is
plausible to interpret its emergent narratives in similar terms as
those of a play session or sports match. To do that, Celia Pearce
provides helpful terminology by introducing six *narrative opera-
tors* (Pearce 2006, 145): experiential, performative, augmentary,
and descriptive elements, as well as metastories and storytelling
systems. This allows, for example, for distinguishing the narrative as experienced by the players themselves (experiential) from
layers of metanarrative information (augmentary), such as back-
stories published on gaming websites. Tying into the previous
section on performativity, the descriptive operator, the "retelling
of description of game events, and the culture that emerges out
of that" (145), has a distinct performative quality, and through
performative retelling these narratives themselves become tools
that inform the game creation process, either as inspiration or
warning signs. For example, the emergency surgery of *Super Meat*

Boy developer Edmund McMillen in 2009, his inability to afford health insurance, and the very high medical costs he faced as a consequence were narrativized—that is, retold—in numerous news reports and online discussions.[22] In these stories, McMillen was framed as a "truly independent" developer, sacrificing both health and financial well-being for his game, and these unusually high stakes likely contributed to the initial spreadability (Ford, Green and Jenkins 2013) of the stories. Moreover, the narrative archetype serves to situate game-making in a larger cultural context, as it exhibits striking similarities with tropes of genius such as those in art music history, which also stylize financial troubles (Richard Wagner or Erik Satie) and failing health (Wolfgang Amadeus Mozart or Frederic Chopin) to position the artist as both "unsettle[ing]" and "ethereal" (Kallberg 1996, ix)—that is, outside everyday life.

As game creation, and the role of tools in it, continues to change, so do the stories that surround and represent it; yet it is not always clear what changes first and what follows suit. Literary scholar Winfried Fluck describes a similarly reciprocal relationship between literature and society as a whole. In his comparative analysis of the American novel, Fluck (1997) interprets literature as a laboratory of societal designs, some of which are not yet feasible and can only exist in the form of fiction. Similarly, the narrativization of game creation blends fact and fiction, thereby contributing to real-world progress rather than "just" documenting it. This function of narratives, which Fluck calls the "cultural imaginary" (in German, *das kulturelle Imaginäre*), can also be traced back to stories like the one about Edmund McMillen, which had a silver lining as both game developers and websites mobilized fans to contribute to the creator's medical costs via PayPal donations.[23] Thus, narrativization here shows but also works toward a potential version of creator-fan relations that is still relatively rare but can become more common in the future.

. . . as an Analytical Process

Playing games is an inherently analytical process: it allows for players to learn about a given subject matter and about themselves. In one of the earliest close readings of a digital game, Ted Friedman (1999) described playing a game as a process of *demystification*, in which "the player molds her or his strategy through trial-and-error experimentation to see 'what works'— which actions are rewarded and which are punished."

Numerous recent independent games consequently analyze pertinent real-world problems through the lens of established, ready-made gameplay systems, essentially using them as tools to shed new light on the underlying issues. For instance, *Papers, Please* (2013) explores the agency of public officials in dictatorial regimes using pattern-matching mechanics, and *Entfremdung* investigates Marx's view on alienation and the division of labor through the lens of an economic simulation game.[24] Understanding game development as a game suggests that the same characteristics apply here as well and that game design tools are always also tools of knowledge production and dissemination.

Yet several of the tool essays in chapter 2 indicate that highly standardized and habitually used tools become increasingly natural, making us increasingly unaware of their existence and their influence on our day-to-day practices. Playful use of tools— such as within the PuzzleScript community, as elaborated in the first section of this chapter—can counter that and reclaim the analytical potential of tools by exploring and pushing their boundaries, even occasionally breaking them in the process. This kind of appropriation also applies to software only peripherally related to game creation, such as 3-D modeling and rendering tools like Autodesk Maya. In his report on the production process of the animated film *Ice Age II*, McEachern (2006) describes examples of technical innovation that clearly exhibit a playful disposition. For example, "character animators challenged one another to a smear-frame competition . . . trying to outdo one another with squash and stretch" poses to create more and more exaggerated character movements and facial features. Upon scaling, rotating and translating the "squash-and-stretch nodes," the corresponding 3-D models were deformed according to an internal physical simulation. Thus, the contest served to playfully analyze the behavior (and limitations) of that simulation. Apart from the competition as a formalized play situation, artists also appropriated and "misused" software created in-house, such as using the newly developed tools to render fur on animals to also design the grass in the valley and tundra scenes, "animating the millions of blades with Fur Follow Through." Literary scholar Bill Brown argues that we "begin to confront the thingness of objects [and specifically tools] when they stop working for us" (Brown 2001, 4). Thus, these calculated dysfunctionalities enable creators to continually reassess the "subject-object relation" (4)—that is, their relationship with the tools at hand. Another important analytical aspect of game creation according to O'Donnell (2009) is "linked to larger systems of experimentation and technoscientific practice." These experiments involve, for example, "artists constantly play[ing] with 3-D models" and engineers looking for creative ways to overcome or compensate for hardware limitations. O'Donnell compares them to navigating a labyrinth, which "cannot be conquered by following a plan" and "force[s] us to move around by means and by virtue of checking out, of groping, of tâtonnement." Thus, as in a game, experimental use of game creation tools involves an ongoing cycle of conceiving and testing hypotheses at every turn.

Tool affordances that facilitate experimentation and analytical approaches to game creation play an important but often overlooked part. The bricolage examples in the eponymous tool essay in chapter 2 present ample evidence of the experimental and analytical potential in game creation tools, but a more detailed look at a simple yet evocative case like that of Bfxr, a web-based tool many independent developers use to create game sound effects, can provide additional insights.[25]

Bfxr allows for creating, storing, and revisiting randomized or mutated (i.e., slightly varied) sounds with a click of a button. This encourages an analytical mindset as designers-as-players may discover interesting sounds and then study (and potentially modify in real time) the parameters to understand how they were produced. To enhance the analytical quality and test hypotheses, users can even lock individual parameters during randomization and compare the results. By providing template sounds labeled Jump or Powerup as a basis for experimentation, Bfxr also enables users to analyze the acoustic characteristics of iconic arcade-style sound effects. The tool further incentivizes curiosity by implementing several hidden features, which are framed as "Secrets" on the website; like knowing about the existence of Easter eggs or secret optional goals in games, these features encourage a more analytical play style.

Apart from software applications, digital prototypes fulfill an important analytical function in game development as well. Referring to John Napier's study of the structure, function, and behavior of the human hand, Mauro (2014) argues that "imagination

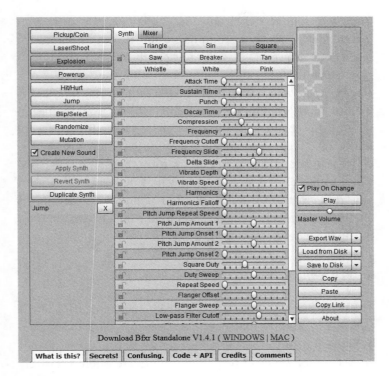

Figure 3.4
Online version of Bfxr (http://bfxr.net).

is basic to tool-making"—that is, making tools both requires and subsequently guides the creator's imagination. Per Mauro, digital prototypes like "all human-made tools start off as chunks of undifferentiated material, which are then shaped according to some cerebral blueprint of what is required." These prototypes are usually not shown, but at PAX East 2012, the developers of *Bastion* (2011) openly demoed the early 2009 prototype of their game, which illustrates its analytical potential.[26] The demo uses placeholder art and only comprises a subset of the final game's mechanics. However, it is already clearly identifiable as *Bastion*, which raises important questions about the "essence" of a game's design and underlying intellectual property (IP). Going back to Turkle's definition of evocative objects from the beginning of this chapter, the prototype helps rationalize aspects of the design, such as parameters of gameplay elements like the dodge roll, and how *Bastion* "started to . . . become a hub-based world with a central location that you come back to"[27] As with any "thing we think with" (Turkle 2007), though, the developers also built an emotional connection to it, which is important for the ongoing development of a game.

. . . as a Communicative Process

The myth of the singular game designer, harkening back to the late 1970s and early 1980s, still occasionally applies today, such as in prominent cases like Daisuke Amaya's *Cave Story* (2004) or Toby Fox's *Undertale* (2015). These games are often intuitively interpreted as a form of communication. For instance, Amaya conveyed a powerful argument about his vision on world-building in games and how retro games could still be relevant in contemporary gaming culture, while Fox communicated his own philosophical ruminations to *Undertale*'s audience not primarily through written language but by tapping into their shared gaming knowledge as a common "code." With these games, the level of craftsmanship or the "quality" of the experience are much less important than connecting with a usually small but well-defined audience and getting across a message or allowing for players to share the creator's perspective.

This particularly applies to autobiographical games (see Werning 2017) like Nicky Case's *Coming Out Simulator* (2014) or Alex Camilleri's *Memoir En Code* (2015).[28] For many people, communicating is a form of introspection and of reaffirming held beliefs and self-conceptions. Similarly, Camilleri describes that making *Memoir En Code* allowed him to rethink and share formative periods of his life by having to "balance . . . both autobiography and open-ended gameplay."[29] That is, he defined his personal anecdotes as a spectrum of gameplay experiences, within which players can have actual agency. The same perspective on making games as self-communication can be applied to other games, like Jason Rohrer's *Passage* (2007) and *Gravitation* (2008) or Anna Anthropy's *Dys4ia* (2012) and *Ohmygod are you alright* (2015). In all these cases, the technical simplicity makes the games effective *tools* for communicating aspects of the self that are difficult to express otherwise. *Escapist Magazine* even commissioned Jason Rohrer to create a "game design sketchbook," which—similar to a diary—enabled him to use games as tools to reflect on and communicate very personal thoughts, such as "feelings about life and death," as well as opinions on social issues like "dealing with police brutality in a public forum."[30]

In most cases, game development itself requires communication on various levels. Affordances for communication are increasingly built into multipurpose software development tools themselves, including "version control, mailing lists [and] additional lightweight collaboration features, such as chat, to increase awareness and support informal communication" (Storey et al. 2010, 359). Apart from communication features in software tools, game creation and the role of tools in it can arguably be characterized as forms of communication in themselves. For instance, in his 2016 Independent Games Summit presentation, programmer Omar Cornut explicitly claims that "tools are communication and that exposing live data to your team [during development] is a strong form of communication" (42'55").[31] He concretizes his approach a bit later, stating that programmers should create small "throwaway tools" (45'15") to "help . . . team members share a common vocabulary" (44'35"). Anna Anthropy and Naomi Clark make a similar point, but from a game design perspective, using language-based metaphors like "vocabulary" (Anthropy and Clark 2014, 1), "verbs and objects" (13), and "conversations" (107) to conceptualize game design. Thus, as suggested in the introduction, game creation can be understood as a dialogue with development tools, and even early game developers cherished the responsiveness of tools. For instance, Janet Murray (1998) argued that by making text-based games that "responded to typed commands" (75) during the 1970s, programmers were "celebrating their pleasure in the increasingly responsive computing environments" (75). Among the—nowadays commonplace—developments that afforded a more "conversational structure between programmer and program" (76) were, for example, human-readable error messages that changed the pacing of (game) programming, affording trial-and-error (or call-and-response) approaches. To make the communicative aspect of game design tools more evocative, it might even be productive to look at tool design in other domains, where the goal of a "dialogue between humans and technology to explore boundaries and creative possibilities" is already more pronounced. For instance, in the context of dance, German design studio Onformative created Pathfinder as a "tool" but also a "visual language to initiate inspiration for choreography."[32] Like how game creation tools can be understood as games themselves, Pathfinder is arguably both a tool and a performance at the same time, generating "geometric shapes and transitions" as inspiration for dancers and, in turn, responding to their movements as input.

Finally, as in previous sections of this chapter, looking beyond Western cultural boundaries can be useful to illustrate the benefits of considering game design as communication. Earlier in this chapter, the creation of military shooter *Special Force 2* was introduced as a performative use and appropriation of Western game development technology. However, the game can also be understood as a response to "recruitainment" games like *America's Army* (2002–) since it mimics (or quotes) many characteristic design elements but notably changes the thematic context to the 2006 Lebanon War between Hezbollah forces and Israel. For example, the game features a "training simulation, where players can practice their shooting skills on targets such as [Ariel] Sharon and other Israeli political and military figures." According to Mahmoud Rayya of the Hezbollah Central Internet Bureau, it was "designed to compete against foreign computer games that show Arabs as enemies."[33] The same principle applies to real-time strategy game *Quraish* (2005), which evokes and thus responds to gameplay elements of the *Age of Empires* franchise (1997–) but shifts the thematic focus to the rise of Islam. The developers claim that "Al-Quraysh is going to help people in the West better understand the people who are living in the East."[34] Thus, unlike *Special Force 2*, *Quraish* is not just a response but explicitly positioned as an invitation to dialogue.

From Production to Distribution: An Outlook

This chapter aimed to use insights from tool analyses to identify essential characteristics of game creation as a process. This is particularly relevant because game design logic is increasingly applied in other areas of contemporary postindustrial societies. For instance, in bottom-up initiatives like the Gezi Jam, a design competition to create simple but persuasive games that address the Turkish government's forcible removal of protesters from Taksim Gezi Park during the 2013 demonstrations, game design rationales were used to inform political protest.[35] The same applies to environmental awareness, communication, and policy-making. For instance, Bengaluru-based game design collective Fields of View aims to inform local and regional policies through board games, and the US National Climate Game Jam encourages small teams to explore issues related to climate change through critical game-making.[36] Thus, more evocative tool design can support not only the five aforementioned ontologies of (entertainment) game creation, but also other cultural practices that rely on game design rationales.

Compared to earlier cultural studies of software tools that focus on one important application, such as Lev Manovich's work on Adobe Photoshop or After Effects, its comparative perspective is one of the key parameters of this book. To study the increasingly fragmented landscape of digital game-making tools, this perspective is necessary, but it can also be productively adapted to other production contexts. Many principles discussed herein also apply in board game design, which increasingly relies on digital technologies to facilitate common tasks but also afford new design experiences. Via Microsoft Excel and Google Sheets, spreadsheets are used to prototype and simulate balancing and gameplay progression patterns.[37] More focused tools like nanDECK, which is aimed at creating playing cards and collectible cards, are even more interesting from a procedural rhetoric angle because they separate the form and content of playing cards.[38]

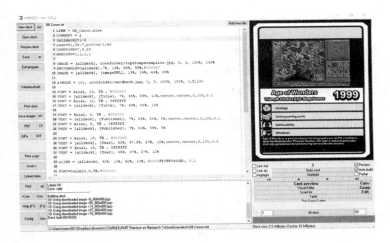

Figure 3.5
Screenshot of nanDECK taken by the author.

All the data that change between cards, such as the labels or the cost to play them, are imported from a spreadsheet, while the design is modified by a simple mark-up language similar to HTML. This structure easily allows for creating entire batches of cards, but it also changes how users perceive a playing card— that is, its ontology.[39] For example, Lev Manovich argues that although an analogue photograph is a configuration of chemicals on photographic film or paper, a digital image, specifically in the Photoshop-specific PSD format, can comprise different image layers and blend modes that can still be manipulated individually, even though they appear as a coherent 2-D image on the computer screen. Similarly, through the lens of nanDECK, the playing card is interpreted as a "container" and a contingent representation for a specific set of data. Nathan Altice puts that argument in historical perspective by interpreting the physical playing card as a "platform" (Altice 2014) that, "materially, . . . is a flat rectangular plane," which can store and organize different types of data. This includes baseball cards, for example, which have been popular collectibles since the early twentieth century, but Altice also mentions more unique examples like the "most wanted" cards, a set of fifty-two playing cards that utilize the regular symbols and numbers but feature images of Iraqi political leaders, with Saddam Hussein as the iconic ace of spades. The set was commissioned and distributed by the US military in 2003 during the invasion of Iraq. Thus, the perception of a playing card as a data type, which blurs the epistemic boundary between analogue and digital games, already existed independently from digital tools. Yet applications like nanDECK now dramatically lower the barriers of entry, effectively enabling anyone to create similar sets. It shifts the status of the playing card from an artifact, manufactured for consumption, toward a material for cultural practice.

Moving past (analogue) game creation, the equally vast array of tools for distributing, selling, and marketing games has been omitted in this book. Yet as both a summary and an outlook on potential follow-up research, this section will briefly illustrate how production and distribution often cannot be neatly separated. Both production and distribution tools have profound implications for our understanding of game genres, formats, or even games themselves as an expressive medium. For example, the concept of independent games, a seemingly homogeneous, widely consensual category of games that allegedly share characteristics with independent film or music, is directly dependent on (digital) distribution channels. Open online marketplaces like Itch.io and self-publishing via social media and specialized services like Gumroad have enabled a sufficiently large number of amateurs to not only make but also share and sell their own games. In the 1980s, games that would today be labeled "independent" used to be disseminated as source code printed in computer game magazines, and readers had to type them into the computer manually. This distribution form distinctly blurred the boundary between making and playing games by using print magazines as a shared dispositif.[40] However, this duality of playing and making is still built into some contemporary tools. For instance, upon starting the first Steam-distributed version of GameMaker: Studio, users saw two large buttons: Play, which allowed for testing game projects shared by others, and Make, which led to the actual editor. These buttons served as a perceived affordance (Norman 1999, 39) because they visually constituted two parts of the same GUI element, two sides of the same coin.

And again, the cultural relevance of this connection can be fruitfully contextualized by tracing it back to reading and writing as two complementary aspects of literacy. Historically, both skills used to be connected—as only those able to write/publish would also habitually read in everyday life; later, they were artificially separated through media-industrial specialization (Kittler 1990), only to be recombined again through contemporary digital writing tools such as Wattpad or Amazon's Write On by Kindle, which enable reading and writing on the same platform. Thus, while truly independent games existed much earlier—for example, Jeff Vogel started his still ongoing *Avernum* series in the 1990s—only digital distribution allowed for them to reach a critical mass, to become visible, and to eventually be perceived by mainstream media as part of a coherent "movement."

In addition, Ian Bogost (2012) hints at how distribution can further alter the ontology of digital games with his remarks on game bundles. Bundles arguably can be conceptualized as tools in two ways. They have a technical component, originally being sold through dedicated websites like Humble Bundle or Indie Royale that required a digital infrastructure to repackage and sell game keys redeemable on partnering platforms like Steam.[41] Yet they are also a conceptual tool in that they can change the way people think about games by offering a new metaphor. For example, Bogost compares game bundles to cereal fun packs, which much earlier began to change children's perception of breakfast cereals, shifting the focus from convenience and nourishment to excitement, sharing, and a sense of discovery.[42] Finally, coming back to one of this book's core themes, the analogy between tool design and game design, several examples already indicate how distribution tools can be playfully used and appropriated. For instance, the game distribution platform Itch.io gives more agency to creators than comparable online marketplaces such as Steam, such as by allowing creators to freely determine and alter the prices of their games. Pricing on Itch.io is evocative in that all games are set to "pay what you want" by default; moreover, the store introduced "pay any amount above the minimum" as a novel product category.[43] Yet independent developer RatCasket co-opted the pricing functionality to implement an uncommon procedural rhetorical strategy on his own profile page, temporarily raising the price of his usually freely distributed games to one hundred dollars.[44]

According to Sicart (2014), this approach can be understood as playful because it reflects an "attitude of play," but "outside the context of play." It still "respects the purposes and goals of [its] object or context" (21); that is, it does not disrupt the purpose of Itch.io as a marketplace, but temporarily challenges its logic in a carnivalesque manner. According to Sicart, playfulness

RatCasket
@RatCasket   (Follow)   ⌄

For a limited time only, all of my games that
are usually free now cost 100 dollars! Wow!
What a deal! Head over to ratcasket.itch.io
and buy some will ya?

Figure 3.6
Independent developer RatCasket announcing the price change for his
games on Itch.io (https://twitter.com/RatCasket/status/10968741555873
66918).

like this enables us to "reambiguate . . . the world" (28), to "see
how the world could be structured as play" (25). In this context,
that means to see how tools could be structured as more diverse,
evocative objects that afford not only productivity but also playfulness, self-expression, and collective discovery.

Acknowledgments

This book outlines a critical perspective on games and (software) tools formulated in conversation with many wonderful people during my time at the universities of Bayreuth and Utrecht since 2014. While writing *Making Games*, I benefited from not only many constructive readers and discussants but also people simply working with or on tools, both in game studies and in other fields like critical data studies. I particularly want to thank Jochen Koubek, with whom I developed the game studies curriculum at the University of Bayreuth, and whose combination of theoretical and practical experience has always been an inspiration. Moreover, I would like to thank Joost Raessens, Michael Mosel, René Glas, Jasper van Vught, Noam Knoller, Hartmut Koenitz, and Daniela van Geenen for valuable insights they provided during various stages of writing.

I am glad that preparing this book allowed me to work with the editors of the Playful Thinking series: Jesper Juul, Mia Consalvo, and particularly William Uricchio and Geoffrey Long, both of whom I first met during my time as a visiting scholar at MIT's Center for Comparative Media Studies in 2005. Collaborating with the MIT Press, in particular Doug Sery and Noah Springer, during the writing of the manuscript has been a fascinating and productive process. Finally, I would like to thank the anonymous reviewers whose feedback helped me make the arguments in this book as accessible and compelling as possible.

This book is for my son Lukas, for whom making games—in *Fortnite* or with pen and paper—is (still) a natural thing to do.

Notes

1 Making Sense of Tools

1. See https://twitter.com/MikeJMika/status/419239296726347776. (The last date of access for this and all following online sources is December 20, 2019).

2. See https://twitter.com/Bob_at_BH/status/419243536551518209.

3. See http://www.wired.com/2015/01/how-twitter-built-a-game-idarb/. The title goes back to Mika's original tweet. The acronym stands for "it draws a red box," and the hashtag refers to the Twitter platform.

4. See https://medium.com/@florentbeauverd/the-social-narrative-of-id arb-outcomes-of-improvisation-in-a-crowdsourced-game-development -c5291ca48f2#.rdh9unvfe.

5. In total, the game went through 133 design stages; see http://please benice.aran-koning.com/allversions.php for an overview of all versions and the suggested features.

6. Because it does not change the game itself, it would be referred to by Gérard Genette as *paratextual*, much like the cover of a book does not change the text but affects how the reader interprets it.

7. Paul Ricoeur called this process *narrative identity formation*, referring to the fact that we construct our personal identity but also our impression of others as stories and try to interpret all the bits and pieces of information we have as part of one consistent "plot."

8. See https://www.youtube.com/watch?v=JeXDNg7scyU.

9. See http://www.wired.com/2013/07/gamelife-video-klax/.

10. For instance, independent developer Jason Rohrer turned to Kickstarter with his already finished game *Diamond Trust of London* because he wanted the game with its highly political and controversial topic to specifically launch on the Nintendo DS, a platform known for family-friendly content. Without Kickstarter, he could not have met Nintendo's large manufacturing minimum. See http://kck.st/1TC5DDe.

11. The director of the Design Lab at the University of California, San Diego, Donald Norman, calls these features *affordances* because they nudge the user toward a specific behavior without explicitly telling or even forcing them to do something (Norman 1999). For instance, in 2013, YouTube tried to incentivize users to comment on videos more considerately by displaying the most upvoted comments at the top of the comments section. The change arguably offered a "prize" for popular comments and, at the same time, made popular comments more easily identifiable, thereby helping users analyze and imitate the underlying strategies effectively.

12. See http://www.windowscentral.com/interview-creator-idarb-xbox-one.

13. See https://unity.com/.

14. See, e.g., http://www.metacritic.com/game/xbox-one/idarb/user-reviews.

15. See, e.g., https://www.gamasutra.com/view/feature/131850/designing_design_tools.php.

16. The studios behind the *Half-Life* franchise and *Second Life*, respectively.

17. See, e.g., https://www.quora.com/What-are-the-best-mobile-application-development-tools and https://www.quora.com/What-are-the-Best-tools-software-for-making-YouTube-videos-for-my-channel.

18. See https://www.gamasutra.com/features/tools-postmortem/.

19. See, e.g., https://www.gamasutra.com/view/feature/131791/the_ana
tomy_of_a_design_document_.php.

20. See, e.g., a movement prototype for the action-adventure game *Ori
and the Blind Forest* (https://www.youtube.com/watch?v=54sAVWoq4nY)
and other videos published by the same account: Moon Game Studios.

21. In that regard, see also Ian Bogost's view on Facebook's and Google's
software engineers, who make the companies' underlying algorithms
appear "mysterious or holy" through constant tweaking (Bogost 2016).

22. See, e.g., http://www.latimes.com/entertainment/herocomplex/la-et
-hc-e3-nintendo-super-mario-graph-paper-drawings-20150617-html
story.html.

23. See https://www.youtube.com/watch?v=Yo7UkkGC1AY&t=157s at
6 min., 43 sec.

24. See, e.g., https://kotaku.com/video-games-helped-me-say-goodbye
-to-my-father-1663956169.

25. See https://www.disneyanimation.com/technology/opensource.

26. See, e.g., https://nofilmschool.com/2014/12/sharegrid-looking-revolu
tionize-way-filmmakers-rent-monetize-their-equipment.

27. See https://eng.uber.com/pyro/.

28. See, e.g., https://medium.com/@raquezha/unity-3d-not-just-games
-aef911e3314c#.86mf6nm9u and https://unity3d.com/showcase/gallery
/non-games.

29. See https://www.assetstore.unity3d.com/en/.

30. See, e.g., http://www.denofgeek.com/us/games/star-wars-fan-games
/234466/star-wars-the-fan-games and https://www.theverge.com/tldr
/2014/11/6/7170213/itc-serif-gothic-is-the-thin-kerned-line-between
-star-wars-the-verge-and-my-childhood.

31. For an illustration, see, e.g., the abundance of videos comparing the
sizes of *Star Wars* vehicles on YouTube, such as https://www.youtube
.com/results?search_query=star+wars+ship+size.

32. See https://3dwarehouse.sketchup.com/search.html?backendClass
=both&q=star%20wars.

33. See http://creatools.gameclassification.com/EN/creatools/index.html
and http://bit.ly/1ROEpIp.

34. For an overview, see, e.g., http://www.filmsite.org/filmchases1.html.

35. See http://ludumdare.com/compo/author/notch/.

36. See, e.g., https://www.polygon.com/2015/12/1/9826622/programmer
-creates-new-xcom-game-in-excel.

37. Consider, for instance, the manifold changes to the piano throughout the nineteenth century, which composers like Franz Liszt closely
followed and took advantage of, thereby extending their own musical
style; http://www.pianosromantiques.com/lisztboisselot.html.

38. The term refers to the material "essence" of a given media format.

39. For a representative set of examples, see, e.g., the PowerPoint shows
hosted by the New York Institute of Technology at http://iris.nyit.edu
/arthistory/pptshows.html.

40. See http://bit.ly/1pHhTV3.

41. The term *dispositif* (with reference to the French philosopher Michel
Foucault) or apparatus is used to describe a standardized viewpoint
associated with a given medium, which has become so common that
it is usually not understood as constructed any more but rather feels
"natural." With respect to cinema, for example, this includes sitting
together with others in a darkened room, looking in the same direction,
and looking at moving images that almost fill the entire view, thereby
disorienting the viewer and promoting the immersion and suspension
of disbelief. See, e.g., http://bit.ly/1WUpOJM.

42. For instance, the technically problematic creation of branching narratives in digital games, which is often aimed at reinforcing the players'
belief in their alleged freedom of choice, is often achieved through tem-
porally branching paths in the game environment rather than by using
other design elements, such as characters.

43. See http://www.deccanchronicle.com/sunday-chronicle/headliners/220516/the-man-who-made-mowgli-s-jungle.html.

44. See https://www.assetstore.unity3d.com/en/#!/content/15641.

45. See http://bit.ly/1l5I8SO.

46. The developers even purchase the most sophisticated modifications, thereby giving their creators a prominent status within the community. See http://bit.ly/1VeHlhS.

47. A version history that allows for retracing which features were added, changed, and removed at which point is accessible at https://unity3d.com/unity/whats-new/.

48. See https://aws.amazon.com/lumberyard/.

49. For an overview of the key differences, see, e.g., http://bit.ly/1V0tEls.

50. Steve Jobs actively intervened in this "conflict" by rejecting support for Adobe Flash content on iOS, claiming that it constituted a security risk and might adversely affect the performance of iPhones. See http://www.apple.com/hotnews/thoughts-on-flash/.

51. Accordingly, the business model arguably becomes a part of the tool's key features (or affordances).

52. See http://recode.net/2015/03/09/it-started-as-a-tweet-now-it-might-be-a-sport-meet-idarb/.

53. See http://www.hookshotinc.com/interview-pop-methodology-experiment-ones-robert-lach/.

54. See http://www.popme1.com/.

55. See http://indiegames.com/2016/08/a_small_robot_story_is_a_platf.html.

56. The name OuLiPo, short for Ouvroir de Literature Potentielle, literally translates as "workshop of potential literature."

57. See, e.g., http://oulipo.net/fr/contraintes/s7.

58. For an overview and explanation of some games, see, e.g., the article by Gray Read at http://bit.ly/1RIWcO7.

59. See http://bit.ly/1V0WTEH for details and an interactive online demo.

60. See https://www.youtube.com/watch?v=dB-CnnasMAQ.

61. The game *How do they do it?* exhibits a very similar strategy, yet applied to a very different subject matter; see http://store.steampowered .com/app/353360/.

62. See, e.g., http://bit.ly/1Lzipz0 and http://bit.ly/1BIuJXf as examples; see, e.g., http://bit.ly/1LCbB3h and http://onforb.es/1UuIvpi.

63. The term *doujin* refers to the Japanese independent game scene, which is generally viewed as a specific subculture and is characterized, for example, by its focus on PC rather than console games, genres like the visual novel, or the *danmaku* (bullet hell) shooter and specialized digital distribution channels.

64. See http://bit.ly/1PDr7Hk.

65. See http://bit.ly/1TZhUkl.

2   Tool Essays

1. See, e.g., the website and corresponding book at https://www.build box.com/.

2. See, e.g., https://www.buildbox.com/forum/index.php?threads/testing -levels.7381/.

3. See http://turtle.audio/.

4. See https://www.youtube.com/watch?v=2YdJa7v99wM and https:// twitter.com/gaohmee/status/960358029911760896.

5. This example from social game company Zynga is discussed on Quora at https://www.quora.com/Which-metrics-does-Zynga-track-on-their-giant -office-dashboards-for-their-social-games.

6. See https://github.com/gephi/gephi/wiki/Datasets.

7. See, e.g., https://blogs.unity3d.com/2018/10/11/now-available-film -sample-project/.

8. See, e.g., https://unity3d.com/learn/tutorials/s/creating-believable-vis uals.

9. See https://docs2.yoyogames.com/source/_build/3_scripting/1_drag _and_drop_overview/changing_dnd.html.

10. O'Donnell (2014) also indicates that even licensed developers used "mod chips" for prototyping "due to the high cost of Nintendo's official developer kits" (742).

11. See https://www.gamasutra.com/view/feature/6214/the_replay_inter views_ralph_baer.php?print=1.

12. See https://forum.yoyogames.com/index.php?threads/game-feel .373/.

13. See http://rdwest.playstation.com/research-technology/phyreengine/.

14. See https://3drealms.com/catalog/ion-maiden_56/.

15. See https://tv.adobe.com/channel/cs-evangelist/.

16. For a profile of Levine and a brief overview of tech evangelism, see https://qz.com/1166041/known-to-fans-as-adobe-jesus-technology -evangelist-jason-levine-takes-software-training-to-a-higher-level/.

17. See, e.g., http://gamemakerblog.com/2009/01/05/5-reasons-why-con struct-is-better-than-game-maker/comment-page-3/.

18. See, e.g., https://www.huffingtonpost.com/entry/the-2016-election -is-secretly-a-game-of-thrones-episode-according-to-the-internet_us _5798dc6ce4b01180b531243c.

19. See https://www.youtube.com/watch?v=W_okgL6HJX8 at 1'47".

20. See https://www.popularmechanics.com/home/tools/a16811/adam -savage-workshop-tour/.

21. See https://www.youtube.com/watch?v=1OPSbF6kM9k at 0'33".

22. See https://www.youtube.com/watch?v=WFu1utKAZ18 at 2′52″.

23. See http://msmemorial.if-legends.org/articles.htm/hc187.php.

24. See https://assetstore.unity.com/. While the UAS is particularly tied to the Unity game engine, there are other platforms, like TurboSquid (for 3-D assets) or GameDev Market, that are tool-agnostic.

25. See https://assetstore.unity.com/packages/tools/level-design/physics-scatter-98305.

26. See https://www.kickstarter.com/projects/inxile/wasteland-2/posts/435142.

27. See, e.g., https://assetstore.unity.com/packages/tools/particles-effects/lens-flares-5.

28. See https://blogs.unity3d.com/2014/02/25/mike-bithell-the-asset-store-is-a-path-to-more-ambitious-indie-games/.

29. See https://marketplace.yoyogames.com/assets/4543/custom-sprite-framework.

30. See https://marketplace.yoyogames.com/assets/450/custom-draw-text.

31. See http://ctrl500.com/game-design/the-puzzle-that-is-puzzle-placement-metricos-solution/.

32. See https://psycnet.apa.org/record/1990-00158-001.

33. See https://medium.com/mammon-machine-zeal/bodies-i-have-in-mind-d84fe23afe13.

34. See https://habbo.fandom.com/wiki/Fridge_Game.

35. One example is the multiplicity of new role-paying games produced every year that closely adhere to the formal and technical limitations of sixteen-bit Japanese role-playing games (because they were created using the RPG Maker tool, which was created in 1992 precisely for that purpose). See http://bit.ly/25uogMt.

36. See https://www.youtube.com/watch?v=4RlpMhBKNr0&t=0h7m57s.

37. See https://www.nevigo.com/en/articydraft/overview/.

38. See https://www.youtube.com/watch?v=h-kifCYToAU at 8'5".

39. See https://www.youtube.com/watch?v=h-kifCYToAU at 17'09".

40. See, e.g., the popularity of the term on Steam: https://www.google. com/search?q=handcrafted+site%3Astore.steampowered.com.

41. See, e.g., https://www.polygon.com/2013/7/8/4502654/spelunky -gamemaker-source-code-available-to-download.

42. See https://store.steampowered.com/tags/en/Character+Customiza tion#p=0&tab=TopSellers.

43. See *Pools of Radiance* as an early example at https://www.youtube .com/watch?v=UaQOVmrjJFA&t=4m56s.

44. See https://www.youtube.com/watch?v=f5GCqcqE7RU.

45. See http://imgur.com/gallery/qGAVO.

46. See https://www.media.mit.edu/publications/edutainment-no-thanks -i-prefer-playful-learning-2/.

47. See, e.g., https://forums.thesims.com/en_US/discussion/769633 /buncha-random-simlebrities.

48. See https://store.steampowered.com/app/668230/SLIFI_2D_Planet _Platformer/.

49. See, e.g., the surprise hit puzzle game *2048* (2014), which spawned its own microgenre.

50. The game was originally titled *Relativity*; see http://www.wired .com/2015/01/relativity-game-development/.

51. See https://archive.org/details/GDC2014Derby.

52. See, e.g., https://gameanalytics.com/blog/how-to-perfect-your-games -core-loop.html.

53. See https://developers.google.com/glass/samples/mini-games.

54. See http://www.gamasutra.com/view/feature/134829/carmack_on _rage.php.

55. See https://kotaku.com/the-most-important-part-of-writing-a-video
-game-is-the-1822627600.

56. See https://www.reddit.com/r/DnD/comments/852gv4/i_couldnt
_find_a_dd_5e_jump_calculator_so_i_made/.

57. See https://www.youtube.com/watch?v=brByJ5EVBn4 at 48′22″.

58. See https://www.youtube.com/watch?v=GZ99gAb4T0o at 14′30″.

59. See, e.g., https://www.youtube.com/watch?v=Kpi4jh96bf0 at 2′35″.

60. See https://www.youtube.com/watch?v=deuVinwv1os at 4′20″.

61. See http://gamasutra.com/blogs/EJRTairne/20130504/176610/The
_Making_and_Unmaking_of_a_GameMaker_Maker.php.

62. See https://gms.yoyogames.com/ReleaseNotes.html.

63. See https://www.yoyogames.com/blog/514/gml-updates-in-2019.

3   A Call for Evocative Tool Design

1. See https://kotaku.com/the-controversy-over-bethesdas-game-engine
-is-misguided-1830435351/.

2. See https://www.youtube.com/watch?v=2YdJa7v99wM.

3. See https://www.gdcvault.com/play/1023235/Keeping-Level-Design
ers-in-the.

4. See http://www.ccs.neu.edu/home/jtpercon/extras/puzzlescript/Doc
umentation/rules101.html.

5. See https://gamejolt.com/games/funky-bird/22273 and http://www
.puzzlescript.net/play.html?p=52dd371d0b74fe1789f8.

6. See https://www.puzzlescript.net/play.html?p=7324598.

7. See, e.g., https://www.youtube.com/watch?v=W_okgL6HJX8 at 24′07″.

8. See https://www.flickgame.org/help.html.

9. These quotes are taken from https://www.reddit.com/r/darksouls /comments/3dvecj/why_i_think_deprived_is_the_best_class_for_new/.

10. The additional rules operate similar to achievements on platforms like Steam, specifying optional goals that yield either in-game rewards or simply social recognition among one's peers. See, e.g., https://global gamejam.org/news/ggj19-diversifiers.

11. See, e.g., http://www.ign.com/articles/2017/04/05/diablo-3-and-the -glorious-return-of-the-necromancer.

12. See, e.g., https://ldjam.com/games. The inclusion of humor especially has been discussed as a contentious but therefore also evocative design choice.

13. See, e.g., https://forum.unity.com/threads/announcement-unearthed -trail-of-ibn-battuta.82755/.

14. See https://www.youtube.com/watch?v=MXLRhUw4FJk.

15. See, e.g., https://www.polygon.com/features/2013/4/24/4257958 /cloned-at-birth-the-story-of-ridiculous-fishing.

16. See https://www.twitch.tv/vlambeer.

17. For an example, see http://getscreenninja.com/videos/henchmen -attack/.

18. For a recent example summarizing the key points in the debate, see https://forum.unity.com/threads/will-dark-theme-be-ever-available-for -free.534612/.

19. See, e.g., https://filmmakermagazine.com/69613-beyond-two-souls -at-the-tribeca-film-festival/.

20. See https://www.youtube.com/watch?v=z5El-yYNUwU. We quote the top comments as of April 7, 2019, but many prominent comments exhibit the same sentiment.

21. See https://www.reddit.com/r/gamedev/comments/4viyth/how_is _this_even_possible_one_person_made_this_in/.

22. See, e.g., http://www.nintendolife.com/news/2009/10/super_meat _boy_developer_hospitalized.

23. See, e.g., http://www.capybaragames.com/2009/10/edmund-mcmil len-maker-of-super-rad-games-needs-help/ and https://www.tigsource .com/2009/10/06/send-edmund-your-love/comment-page-1/.

24. See https://colestia.itch.io/entfremdung.

25. See https://www.bfxr.net/ or https://iznaut.itch.io/bfxr.

26. See https://www.youtube.com/watch?v=7NkMvqtaAW0.

27. See https://www.youtube.com/watch?v=7NkMvqtaAW0 for a video demonstration of the Bastion prototype; the quote starts at around 2′52″.

28. See http://www.memoirencode.com/

29. See https://www.gamasutra.com/view/news/282312/Autobiograph ical_Memoir_En_Code_finds_game_mechanics_in_daily_life.php.

30. See https://v1.escapistmagazine.com/articles/view/video-games/col umns/gamedesignsketchbook.

31. See https://www.youtube.com/watch?v=W_okgL6HJX8.

32. See http://prix2016.aec.at/prixwinner/19657/.

33. See https://www.wnd.com/2003/03/17550/.

34. See, e.g., http://www.csmonitor.com/2006/0605/p07s02-wome.html.

35. See https://twitter.com/hashtag/GeziJAM for a backlog of Twitter communications around the event.

36. See, e.g., the work of the Fields of View team in Bengaluru, India, to gamify policymaking at https://factordaily.com/gamify-policymak ing-civic-issues-bengaluru-fields-of-view/. For the US National Climate Game Jam, see https://www.climate.gov/teaching/professional-develop ment/national-climate-game-jam.

37. See, e.g., http://rubycowgames.com/excel-and-google-docs-spread sheet-tips-for-game-designers/.

38. See http://www.nand.it/nandeck/.

39. See the introduction for more details on how tools affect the ontology of media as (physical or digital) artifacts.

40. The term is used here according to Hickethier's (1995) definition—that is, to describe a partly standardized set of material conditions that characterize how we engage with a medium. In Hickethier's case, he described the role of the television set as a central object in the living room.

41. See https://archive.is/20130619212226/http://www.indieroyale.com/bundle.

42. See http://www.gamasutra.com/view/feature/134962/persuasive_games_what_is_a_game_.php.

43. See https://itch.io/docs/creators/pricing.

44. See https://twitter.com/RatCasket/status/1096874155587366918.

References

Aarseth, Espen. 2003. "Playing Research: Methodological Approaches to Game Analysis." In *Proceedings of the Digital Arts and Culture Conference.* http://heim.ifi.uio.no/~gisle/ifi/aarseth.pdf.

Agazzi, Evandro. 1998. "From Technique to Technology: The Role of Modern Science." *Techné: Research in Philosophy and Technology* 4 (2). http://scholar.lib.vt.edu/ejournals/SPT/v4n2/AGAZZI.html.

Ahmed, Sara. 2004. "Affective Economies." *Social Text* 22 (2): 117–139.

Altice, Nathan. 2014. "The Playing Card Platform." *Analog Game Studies* 4 (2). http://analoggamestudies.org/2014/11/the-playing-card-platform/.

Anthropy, Anna, and Naomi Clark. 2014. *A Game Design Vocabulary: Exploring the Foundational Principles behind Good Game Design.* Upper Saddle River, NJ: Addison-Wesley.

Bainbridge, Wilma Alice, and William Sims Bainbridge. 2007. "Creative Uses of Software Errors: Glitches and Cheats." *Social Science Computer Review* 25 (1): 61–77. https://doi.org/10.1177/0894439306289510.

Bal, Mieke. 2013. "Imaging Madness: Inter-ships." *InPrint* 2 (1): 51–70. http://arrow.dit.ie/inp/vol2/iss1/5.

Banks, Miranda, Bridget Conor, and Vicki Mayer, eds. 2016. *Production Studies, the Sequel! Cultural Studies of Global Media Industries.* New York: Routledge.

Barthes, Roland. 2006. "Myth Today." In *Cultural Theory and Popular Culture: A Reader*, vol. 1, 3rd ed., edited by John Storey, 293–302. Harlow, UK: Pearson Education.

Batty, Michael. 2015. "A Perspective on City Dashboards." *Regional Studies, Regional Science* 2 (1): 29–32.

Becker, Howard S. 1982. *Art Worlds*. Berkeley: University of California Press.

Benkwitz, Adam, and Gyozo Molnar. 2012. "Interpreting and Exploring Football Fan Rivalries: An Overview." *Soccer and Society* 13 (4): 479–494. https://doi.org/10.1080/14660970.2012.677224.

Binder, Thomas, Giorgio De Michelis, Pelle Ehn, Giulio Jacucci, Per Linde, and Ina Wagner. 2011. *Design Things*. Cambridge, MA: MIT Press.

Birdwell, Ken. 1999. "The Cabal: Valve's Design Process for Creating Half-Life." *Gamasutra* (blog). December 10, 1999. http://www.gamasutra .com/view/feature/3408/the_cabal_valves_design_process_.php.

Bizzocchi, Jim. 2007. "Games and Narrative: An Analytical Framework." *Loading: The Journal of the Canadian Game Studies Association* 1 (1): 5–10.

Boell, Sebastian K., and Florian Hoof. 2015. "Using Heider's Epistemology of Thing and Medium for Unpacking the Conception of Documents: Gantt Charts and Boundary Objects." *Proceedings from the Document Academy* 2 (1). http://ideaexchange.uakron.edu/docam/vol2/iss1/3.

Bogost, Ian. 2007. *Persuasive Games: The Expressive Power of Videogames*. Cambridge, MA: MIT Press.

Bogost, Ian. 2008. "The Rhetoric of Video Games." In *The Ecology of Games: Connecting Youth, Games, and Learning*, edited by Katie Salen, 117–140. Cambridge, MA: MIT Press.

Bogost, Ian. 2012. "What Is a Game Bundle?" *Gamasutra* (blog). January 19, 2012. http://www.gamasutra.com/view/feature/6595/persuasive_games _what_is_a_game_.php.

Bogost, Ian. 2016. "Go Tweak Yourself, Facebook." *Atlantic*, April 28, 2016. http://www.theatlantic.com/technology/archive/2016/04/go-tweak -yourself-facebook/480258/.

Bogost, Ian, and Nick Montfort. 2007. "New Media as Material Constraint: An Introduction to Platform Studies." Paper presented at the 1st International HASTAC Conference, Duke University, Durham, NC, April 19–21. http://bogost.com/downloads/Bogost Montfort HASTAC.pdf.

Bolter, Jay David. 2001. *Writing Space: Computers, Hypertext, and the Remediation of Print.* New York: Routledge.

Bourdaa, Mélanie. 2013. "'Following the Pattern': The Creation of an Encyclopaedic Universe with Transmedia Storytelling." *Adaptation* 6 (2): 202–214. https://doi.org/10.1093/adaptation/apt009.

Brandt, Eva. 2006. "Designing Exploratory Design Games." In *Proceedings of the Ninth Conference on Participatory Design: Expanding Boundaries in Design—PDC '06*, vol. 1, 57–66. New York: ACM Press. https://doi.org/10.1145/1147261.1147271.

Brown, Bill. 2001. "Thing Theory." *Critical Inquiry* 28 (1): 1–22. https://doi.org/10.1086/449030.

Burwell, Catherine, and Thomas Miller. 2016. "Let's Play: Exploring Literacy Practices in an Emerging Videogame Paratext." *E-Learning and Digital Media* 13 (3–4): 109–125.

Byerly, Alison. 1999. "Effortless Art: The Sketch in Nineteenth-Century Painting and Literature." *Criticism* 41 (3): 349–364.

Cage, David. 2006. "Indigo Prophecy: The Nightmare of the Original Concept." *Game Developer*, June 2006.

Caillois, Roger, and Elaine P. Halperin. 1955. "The Structure and Classification of Games." *Diogenes* 3 (62): 62–75. https://doi.org/10.1126/science.9.215.212.

Caldwell, John Thornton. 2004. "Modes of Production: The Televisual Apparatus." In *The Television Studies Reader*, edited by Robert C. Allen and Annette Hill, 293–310. New York: Routledge.

Caperton, Idit Harel. 2012. "Toward a Theory of Game-Media Literacy: Playing and Building as Reading and Writing." In *Interdisciplinary Advancements in Gaming, Simulations and Virtual Environments: Emerging*

Trends: Emerging Trends, edited by Richard E. Ferdig and Sara de Freitas, 1–17. Hershey, PA: IGI Global.

Chapple, Craig. 2012. "Unity Focus." *Develop*, June 2012, 52.

Chen, Jenova. 2007. "Flow in Games (and Everything Else)." *Communications of the ACM* 50 (4): 31–34.

Chen, Robert, and Jeanny Liu. 2015. "Personas: Powerful Tool for Designers." In *Design Thinking: New Product Development Essentials from the PDMA*, edited by Michael G. Luchs, K. Scott Swan, and Abbie Griffin, 27–40. Hoboken, NJ: John Wiley & Sons, Inc. https://doi.org /10.1002/9781119154273.ch3.

Choi, Mary H. K. 2011. "In Praise of Binge TV Consumption." *WIRED*, December 27, 2011. https://www.wired.com/2011/12/pl_column_tv series/.

Consalvo, Mia. 2007. *Cheating: Gaining Advantage in Videogames*. Cambridge, MA: MIT Press.

Crawford, Chris. 2003. *On Game Design*. Berkeley, CA: New Riders.

Cubitt, Sean. 1999. "Phalke, Melies, and Special Effects Today." *Wide Angle* 21 (1): 115–130.

Culkin, John. 1967. "A Schoolman's Guide to Marshall McLuhan." *Saturday Review*, March 1967.

Curinga, Matthew X. 2014. "Critical Analysis of Interactive Media with Software Affordances." *First Monday* 19 (9). http://firstmonday.org/ojs /index.php/fm/article/view/4757/4116.

Deuze, Mark. 2006. "Participation, Remediation, Bricolage: Considering Principal Components of a Digital Culture." *Information Society* 22 (2): 63–75. https://doi.org/10.1080/01972240600567170.

Draxler, Sebastian, Gunnar Stevens, Martin Stein, Alexander Boden, and David Randall. 2012. "Supporting the Social Context of Technology Appropriation: On a Synthesis of Sharing Tools and Tool Knowledge." In *Proceedings of the 2012 ACM Annual Conference on Human Factors in*

Computing Systems—CHI '12, 2835–2844. New York: ACM Press. https://doi.org/10.1145/2207676.2208687.

Eco, Umberto. 1977. "Semiotics of Theatrical Performance." *Drama Review* 21 (1): 107–117. http://www.jstor.org/stable/1145112.

Fischer-Lichte, Erika. 2008. *The Transformative Power of Performance: A New Aesthetics*. London: Routledge.

Fluck, Winfried. 1997. Das Kulturelle Imaginäre: Funktionsgeschichte Des Amerikanischen Romans, 1790–1900. Frankfurt: Suhrkamp.

Ford, Sam, Joshua Green, and Henry Jenkins. 2013. Spreadable Media: Creating Value and Meaning in a Networked Culture. New York: NYU Press.

Friedman, Batya. 1996. "Value-Sensitive Design." *Interactions* 3 (6): 16–23. https://doi.org/10.1145/242485.242493.

Friedman, Ted. 1999. "The Semiotics of SimCity." *First Monday* 4 (4). https://doi.org/10.5210/fm.v4i4.660.

Gardien, Paul, Tom Djajadiningrat, Caroline Hummels, and Aarnout Brombacher. 2014. "Changing Your Hammer: The Implications of Paradigmatic Innovation for Design Practice." *International Journal of Design* 8 (2): 119–139.

Geertz, Clifford. 1972. "Deep Play: Notes on the Balinese Cockfight." *Daedalus* 101 (1): 1–37.

Gillespie, Tarleton. 2017. "The Platform Metaphor, Revisited." *HIIG Science* (blog). August 24, 2017. https://www.hiig.de/en/blog/the-platform-metaphor-revisited/.

Goetz, Thomas. 2011. "Harnessing the Power of Feedback Loops." *WIRED*, June 19, 2011. https://www.wired.com/2011/06/ff_feedbackloop/.

Goussencourt, Timothée De, and Pascal Bertolino. 2015. "Using the Unity Game Engine as a Platform for Advanced Real Time Cinema Image Processing." Paper presented at the International Conference on Image Processing (ICIP), Québec, Canada, September. https://hal.archives-ouvertes.fr/hal-01208180v2/document.

Graaf, Shenja van der. 2012. "Get Organized at Work! A Look Inside the Game Design Process of Valve and Linden Lab." *Bulletin of Science Technology Society* 32 (6): 480–488.

Graaf, Shenja van der. 2017. *ComMODify: User Creativity at the Intersection of Commerce and Community*. Cham: Palgrave Macmillan.

Gruzd, Anatoliy, Barry Wellman, and Yuri Takhteyev. 2011. "Imagining Twitter as an Imagined Community." *American Behavioral Scientist* 55 (10): 1294–1318. https://doi.org/10.1177/0002764211409378.

Guevara-Villalobos, Orlando. 2011. "Cultures of Independent Game Production: Examining the Relationship between Community and Labour." In *Think Design Play: The Fifth International Conference of the Digital Research Association (DIGRA)*. Hilversum, NL: [online]. www.digra .org/dl/db/11307.08157.pdf.

Heidenreich, Stefan. 2004. *FlipFlop. Digitale Datenströme Und Die Kultur Des 21. Jahrhunderts*. München: Carl Hansen Verlag.

Hickethier, Knut. 1995. "Dispositiv Fernsehen. Skizze Eines Modells." *Montage/AV* 4 (1): 63–84.

Horwatt, Eli. 2009. "A Taxonomy of Digital Video Remixing: Contemporary Found Footage Practice on the Internet." In *Cultural Borrowings: Appropriation, Reworking, Transformation*, edited by Iain Robert Smith, 76–91. Nottingham, UK: *Scope: An Online Journal of Film and Television Studies*. http://clublum.com/images/Scope-Cultural_Borrowings_Final% 20clublum.pdf.

James, Alison. 2009. *Constraining Chance: Georges Perec and the Oulipo*. Evanston, IL: Northwestern University Press.

Jansen, Slinger, Anthony Finkelstein, and Sjaak Brinkkemper. 2009. "A Sense of Community: A Research Agenda for Software Ecosystems." In *ICSE-Companion 2009: 31st International Conference on Software Engineering*, 187–190. Vancouver, BC: IEEE. http://ieeexplore.ieee.org/xpls/abs _all.jsp?arnumber=5070978.

Jenkins, Henry. 2006. *Convergence Culture: Where Old and New Media Collide*. New York: New York University Press.

Jenkins, Henry. 2007. "Narrative Spaces." In *Space Time Play*, edited by Friedrich von Borries, Steffen P. Walz, and Matthias Böttger, 56–60. Basel, Boston & Berlin: Birkhäuser.

Jenkins, Henry. 2009. "Spoiling Survivor: The Anatomy of a Knowledge Community." In *Convergence Culture: Where Old and New Media Collide*, edited by Henry Jenkins, 25–58. New York: New York University Press.

Jenkins, Henry. 2014. "Rethinking 'Rethinking Convergence/Culture.'" *Cultural Studies* 28 (2): 267–297. https://doi.org/10.1080/09502386.2013.801579.

Jones, Ian Bryce. 2016. "Do the Locomotion: Obstinate Avatars, Dehiscent Performances, and the Rise of the Comedic Video Game." *Velvet Light Trap* 77 (March): 86–99. https://doi.org/10.7560/vlt7706.

Kallberg, Jeffrey. 1996. *Chopin at the Boundaries: Sex, History, and Musical Genre*. Cambridge, MA: Harvard University Press.

Katharine, Neil. 2012. "Game Design Tools: Time to Evaluate." Paper presented at the *2012 International Nordic DiGRA Conference*, Tampere, Finland, June 6–8. http://www.digra.org/wp-content/uploads/digital-library/12168.46494.pdf.

Kattenbelt, Chiel. 2010. "Intermediality in Performance and as a Mode of Performativity." In *Mapping Intermediality in Performance*, edited by Sarah Bay-Cheng, Chiel Kattenbelt, Andy Lavender, and Robin Nelson, 29–37. Amsterdam: Amsterdam University Press.

Keim, Brandon. 2010. "Your Computer Really Is a Part of You." *WIRED*, March 9, 2010. https://www.wired.com/2010/03/heidegger-tools/.

Keith, Clinton. 2010. *Agile Game Development with Scrum*. Boston, MA: Addison-Wesley Professional.

Kittler, Friedrich A. 1990. *Discourse Networks 1800/1900*. Stanford, CA: Stanford University Press.

Koszarski, Richard. 1990. *An Evening's Entertainment: The Age of the Silent Feature Picture, 1915–1928*. Berkeley: University of California Press.

Latour, Bruno. 2007. *Reassembling the Social: An Introduction to Actor-Network-Theory*. Oxford: Oxford University Press.

Lehmann, Ann-Sophie. 2012. "Taking the Lid off the Utah Teapot: The Materials of Computer Graphics." *Zeitschrift Für Medien Und Kulturforschung*, January: 157–172.

Leigh Star, Susan. 2010. "This Is Not a Boundary Object: Reflections on the Origin of a Concept." *Science, Technology, & Human Values* 35 (5): 601–617. https://doi.org/10.1177/0162243910377624.

Lessard, Jonathan. 2009. "Fahrenheit and the Premature Burial of Interactive Movies." *Eludamos: Journal for Computer Game Culture* 3 (2): 195–205. http://www.eludamos.org/index.php/eludamos/article/view /vol3no2-5/130.

Loring-Albright, Greg. 2015. "The First Nations of Catan: Practices in Critical Modification." *Analog Game Studies* 2 (7). http://analoggame studies.org/2015/11/the-first-nations-of-catan-practices-in-critical-mod ification/.

Louridas, Panagiotis. 1999. "Design as Bricolage: Anthropology Meets Design Thinking." *Design Studies* 20 (6): 517–535. https://doi.org/10.1016 /S0142-694X(98)00044-1.

Loyer, Erik. 2010. "Stories as Instruments." *Television & New Media* 11 (3): 180–196.

Manovich, Lev. 2001. *The Language of New Media*. Cambridge, MA: MIT Press.

Manovich, Lev. 2007. "After Effects, or Velvet Revolution." *Artifact* 1 (2): 67–75.

Manovich, Lev. 2011. "Inside Photoshop." *Computational Culture* 1 (1). http://computationalculture.net/article/inside-photoshop.

Manovich, Lev. 2013. *Software Takes Command*. New York: Bloomsbury. https://issuu.com/bloomsburypublishing/docs/9781623566722_web.

Martin, Chase Bowen, and Mark Deuze. 2009. "The Independent Production of Culture: A Digital Games Case Study." *Games and Culture* 4 (3): 276–295. https://doi.org/10.1177/1555412009339732.

Mauro, Aaron. 2014. "'To Think a World without Thought': Negotiating Speculative Realism in a Digital Humanities Practice." *Digital Studies/Le Champ Numérique* 5 (1). https://doi.org/10.16995/dscn.52.

Mayer, Vicki, Miranda J. Banks, and John Thornton Caldwell. 2009. *Production Studies: Cultural Studies of Media Industries.* New York: Routledge.

McArthur, Victoria, Robert John Teather, and Jennifer Jenson. 2015. "The Avatar Affordances Framework: Mapping Affordances and Design Trends in Character Creation Interfaces." In *Proceedings of the 2015 Annual Symposium on Computer-Human Interaction in Play*, 231–240. New York: ACM. https://doi.org/10.1145/2793107.2793121.

McEachern, Martin. 2006. "Thawsome: Fox/Blue Sky Bring a Flood of Innovation to Ice Age: The Meltdown." *Computer Graphics World* 29 (4): 12–18.

McLuhan, Marshall. 1994. *Understanding Media: The Extensions of Man.* Cambridge, MA: MIT Press.

McMillan, Robert. 2013. "From Collaborative Coding to Wedding Invitations: GitHub Is Going Mainstream." *WIRED*, September 2, 2013. https://www.wired.com/2013/09/github-for-anything/.

Menzel, Donald H. 1968. "Doodling as a Form of Art." *Leonardo* 1 (2): 175–177.

Miettinen, Reijo. 1999. "The Riddle of Things: Activity Theory and Actor-Network Theory as Approaches to Studying Innovations." *Mind, Culture, and Activity* 6 (3): 170–195. http://www.tandfonline.com/doi/abs/10.1080/10749039909524725.

Mittell, Jason. 2006. "Narrative Complexity in Contemporary American Television." *Velvet Light Trap* 58 (1): 29–40.

Montfort, Nick, and Ian Bogost. 2009. *Racing the Beam: The Atari Video Computer System.* Cambridge, MA: MIT Press.

Murray, Janet. 1997. *Hamlet on the Holodeck: The Future of Narrative in Cyberspace.* New York: Free Press.

Newman, Michael Z. 2006. "From Beats to Arcs: Toward a Poetics of Television Narrative." *Velvet Light Trap* 58 (1): 16–28.

Nideffer, Robert F. 2011. "Game Engines as Creative Frameworks." In *Context Providers: Conditions of Meaning in Media Arts*, edited by Margot Lovejoy, Christiane Paul, and Victoria Vesna, 175–197. Bristol: Intellect.

Nieborg, David B., and Shenja Van der Graaf. 2008. "The Mod Industries? The Industrial Logic of Non-market Game Production." *European Journal of Cultural Studies* 11 (2): 177–195.

Niederer, Sabine, and José van Dijck. 2010. "Wisdom of the Crowd or Technicity of Content? Wikipedia as a Sociotechnical System." *New Media & Society* 12 (8): 1368–1387.

Norman, Donald A. 1999. "Affordance, Conventions, and Design." *Interactions* 6 (3): 38–43. https://doi.org/10.1145/301153.301168.

Nutt, Christian. 2012. "Beyond Heavy Rain: David Cage on Interactive Narrative." *Gamasutra* (blog). May 25, 2012. http://www.gamasutra.com /view/feature/171004/beyond_heavy_rain_david_cage_on_.php.

O'Donnell, Casey. 2009. "The Everyday Lives of Video Game Developers: Experimentally Understanding Underlying Systems/Structures." *Transformative Works and Cultures* 2 (1). http://dx.doi.org/10.3983/twc .2009.0073.

O'Donnell, Casey. 2014a. *Developer's Dilemma: The Secret World of Videogame Creators*. Cambridge, MA: MIT Press.

O'Donnell, Casey. 2014b. "Mixed Messages: The Ambiguity of the MOD Chip and Pirate Cultural Production for the Nintendo DS." *New Media and Society* 16 (5): 737–752.

Orlikowski, Wanda J. 2007. "Sociomaterial Practices: Exploring Technology at Work." *Organization Studies* 28 (9): 1435–1448. https://doi.org /10.1177/0170840607081138.

O'Shaughnessy, Hilary, and Nicholas Ward. 2014. "The Use of Physical Theatre Improvisation in Game Design." In *Proceedings of the 8th Nordic Conference on Human-Computer Interaction Fun, Fast, Foundational— NordiCHI '14*, 588–597. New York: ACM Press.

Owens, Craig. 1980. "The Allegorical Impulse: Toward a Theory of Post-modernism." *October* 12:67–86.

Parkin, Lance. 2009. "Truths Universally Acknowledged: How the 'Rules' of Doctor Who Affect the Writing." In *Third Person: Authoring and Exploring Vast Narratives*, edited by Noah Wardrip-Fruin and Pat Harrigan, 13–24. Cambridge, MA: MIT Press.

Pearce, Celia. 2006. "Towards a Game Theory of Game." In *First Person: New Media as Story, Performance, and Game*, edited by Noah-Wardrip Fruin and Pat Harrigan, 143–153. Cambridge, MA: MIT Press.

Peppler, Kylie A., and Yasmin B. Kafai. 2007. "What Videogame Making Can Teach Us about Literacy and Learning: Alternative Pathways into Participatory Culture." In *DiGRA '07—Proceedings of the 2007 DiGRA International Conference: Situated Play*, vol. 4, 369–376. Tokyo: University of Tokyo. http://www.digra.org/digital-library/publications/what-video game-making-can-teach-us-about-literacy-and-learning-alternative -pathways-into-participatory-culture/.

Pias, Claus. 2009. "'electronic Overheads' Elemente Einer Vorgeschichte von PowerPoint." In *Powerpoint. Macht Und Einfluss Eines Präsentationsprogramms*, edited by Wolfgang Coy and Claus Pias, 16–44. Frankfurt: Fischer Taschenbuch Verlag.

Pias, Claus, and Wolfgang Coy, eds. 2009. *PowerPoint: Macht Und Einfluss Eines Präsentationsprogramms*. Frankfurt: Fischer Taschenbuch Verlag.

Riede, Felix, Niels N. Johannsen, Anders Högberg, April Nowell, and Marlize Lombard. 2018. "The Role of Play Objects and Object Play in Human Cognitive Evolution and Innovation." *Evolutionary Anthropology* 27 (1): 46–59. https://doi.org/10.1002/evan.21555.

Rieder, Bernhard, and Theo Röhle. 2012. "Digital Methods: Five Challenges." In *Understanding Digital Humanities*, edited by David M. Berry, 67–84. Basingstoke: Palgrave Macmillan.

Rogers, Matt. 2012. "Contextualizing Theories and Practices of Bricolage Research." *Qualitative Report* 17 (48): 1–17. http://nsuworks.nova.edu/tqr /vol17/iss48/3.

Rosmarin, Rachel. 2006. "The MySpace Economy." *Forbes*, April 10, 2006. http://www.forbes.com/2006/04/07/myspace-google-murdoch-cx _rr_0410myspace.html.

Salen, Katie, and Eric Zimmerman. 2004. *Rules of Play: Game Design Fundamentals*. Cambridge, MA: MIT Press.

Salovaara, Antti. 2008. "Inventing New Uses for Tools: A Cognitive Foundation for Studies on Appropriation." *Human Technology: An Interdisciplinary Journal on Humans in ICT Environments* 4 (2): 209–228.

Salter, Anastasia, and John Murray. 2014. "Marking New Ground: Flash, HTML5 and the Future of the Web Arcade." Paper presented at *the 9th International Conference on the Foundations of Digital Games (FDG)*, Royal Caribbean's Liberty of the Seas, April 3–7. http://www.fdg2014.org /papers/fdg2014_paper_27.pdf.

Schell, Jesse. 2014. *The Art of Game Design: A Book of Lenses*. 2nd ed. Boca Raton, FL: CRC Press.

Schepelern, Peter. 2005. "The Making of an Auteur." In *Visual Authorship: Creativity and Intentionality in Media*, edited by Torben Kragh Grodal, Bente Larsen, and Iben Thorving Laursen, 103–128. Copenhagen: Museum Tusculanum.

Sefelin, Reinhard, Manfred Tscheligi, and Verena Giller. 2003. "Paper Prototyping—What Is It Good for? A Comparison of Paper- and Computer-Based Low-Fidelity Prototyping." In *CHI '03 Extended Abstracts on Human Factors in Computing Systems*, 778–779. New York: ACM. https://doi.org/10.1145/765891.765986.

Sicart, Miguel. 2014. *Play Matters*. Cambridge, MA: MIT Press.

Silver, Alain. 1996. "Son of Noir: Neo-Film Noir and the Neo-B Picture." In *Film Noir Reader*, edited by Alain Silver and James Ursini, 331–338. New York: Limelight Editions.

Simons, Jan. 2007. *Playing the Waves: Lars von Trier's Game Cinema*. Amsterdam: Amsterdam University Press.

Sismondo, Sergio. 2011. *An Introduction to Science and Technology Studies*. Malden, MA: John Wiley & Sons.

Smith, Tim J. 2014. "Audiovisual Correspondences in Sergei Eisenstein's Alexander Nevsky: A Case Study in Viewer Attention." In *Cognitive Media Theory*, edited by Ted Nanicelli and Paul Taberham, 85–105. New York: Routledge.

Sotamaa, Olli. 2009. "Game Achievements, Collecting and Gaming Capital." In *Future and Reality of Games*, edited by Konstantin Mitgutsch, Christoph Klimmt, and Herbert Rosenstingl, 239–250. Vienna: Braumüller.

Sotamaa, Olli. 2010. "When the Game Is Not Enough: Motivations and Practices among Computer Game Modding Culture." *Games and Culture* 5 (3): 239–255. https://doi.org/10.1177/1555412009359765.

Spinellis, Diomidis. 2005. "Tool Writing: A Forgotten Art?" *IEEE Software* 22 (4): 9–11. https://doi.org/10.1109/MS.2005.111.

Stabell, Charles B., and Øystein D. Fjeldstad. 1998. "Configuring Value for Competitive Advantage: On Chains, Shops and Networks." *Strategic Management Journal* 19:413–437.

Stanfill, Mel. 2015. "The Interface as Discourse: The Production of Norms through Web Design." *New Media & Society* 17 (7): 1059–1074. https://doi.org/10.1177/1461444814520873.

Stones, Catherine, and Tom Cassidy. 2007. "Comparing Synthesis Strategies of Novice Graphic Designers Using Digital and Traditional Design Tools." *Design Studies* 28 (1): 59–72. https://doi.org/10.1016/j.destud.2006.09.001.

Storey, Margaret-Anne, Christoph Treude, Arie van Deursen, and Li-Te Cheng. 2010. "The Impact of Social Media on Software Engineering Practices and Tools." In *Proceedings of the FSE/SDP Workshop on the Future of Software Engineering Research*, 359–364. New York: ACM.

Sturm, Damion, and Andrew McKinney. 2013. "Affective Hyperconsumption and Immaterial Labors of Love: Theorizing Sport Fandom in the Age of New Media." *Participations* 10 (1): 357–362.

Su, Chih Sheng, and Rung Huei Liang. 2013. "Designing for Resonance by Evocative Objects: An Experiential Interaction Design Method."

In *Lecture Notes in Computer Science (Including Subseries Lecture Notes in Artificial Intelligence and Lecture Notes in Bioinformatics)*, 610–619. Berlin: Springer. https://doi.org/10.1007/978-3-642-39229-0_65.

Suits, Bernard. 1967. "What Is a Game?" *Philosophy of Science* 34 (2): 148–156.

Sullivan, J. L. 2009. "Leo C. Rosten's Hollywood: Power, Status, and the Primacy of Social Networks in Cultural Production." In *Production Studies: Cultural Studies of Media Industries*, edited by Vicki Mayer, Miranda J. Banks, and John Thornton Caldwell, 39–53. New York: Routledge.

Suwa, Masaki, and Barbara Tversky. 1996. "What Architects See in Their Sketches." In *Conference Companion on Human Factors in Computing Systems Common Ground—CHI '96*, 191–192. New York: ACM Press. https://doi.org/10.1145/257089.257255.

Teurlings, Jan. 2013. "Unblackboxing Production: What Media Studies Can Learn from Actor-Network Theory." In *After the Break: Television Theory Today*, edited by Marijke de Valck and Jan Teurlings, 101–116. Amsterdam: Amsterdam University Press.

Thompson, Clive. 2002. "Dot-Columnist: Online Video Games Are the Newest Form of Social Comment." *Slate*, August 29, 2002. http://www.slate.com/articles/technology/webhead/2002/08/dotcolumnist.html.

Thompson, Clive. 2012. "How Social Media Turns Creative Pursuits Into 'Live' Performances." *WIRED*, July 26, 2012. https://www.wired.com/2012/07/st-thompson-social-media/.

Thomsen, Michael. 2013. "Beyond: Two Souls Woos Movie-Goers at Tribeca Film Festival." *IGN*, May 3, 2013. http://www.ign.com/articles/2013/05/03/beyond-two-souls-woos-movie-goers-at-tribeca-film-festival.

Treanor, Mike, and Michael Mateas. 2011. "BurgerTime: A Proceduralist Investigation." Paper presented at the *DiGRA 2011 Conference: Think Design Play*, Hilversum, Netherlands, September 14–17. http://www.digra.org/digital-library/publications/burgertime-a-proceduralist-investigation/.

Turkle, Sherry. 2007. *Evocative Objects: Things We Think With*. Cambridge, MA: MIT Press.

Tuunanen, Janne, and Juho Hamari. 2012. "Meta-Synthesis of Player Typologies." Paper presented at the *Nordic Digra 2012 Conference: Local and Global—Games in Culture and Society*, Tampere, Finland, June 6–8. http://www.digra.org/wp-content/uploads/digital-library/12168.40312.pdf.

Vanderhoef, John, and Michael Curtin. 2016. "The Crunch Heard Round the World: The Global Era of Digital Game Labor." In *Production Studies: The Sequel*, edited by Bridget Conor, Miranda Banks, and Vicki Mayer, 196–210. New York: Routledge.

Vdovychenko, Nataliia, and Carmen Gabriela Lupu. 2018. "Plastic Surgery and the Quest for the Perfect Selfie in South Korea." *Diggit Magazine*, November 26, 2018. https://www.diggitmagazine.com/articles/plastic-surgery-quest-perfect-selfie-south-korea.

Werning, Stefan. 2017. "The Persona in Autobiographical Game-Making as a Playful Performance of the Self." *Persona Studies* 3 (1): 28–42.

Werning, Stefan. 2018a. "Conceptualizing Game Distribution: Kickstarter and the Board Game 'Renaissance.'" *La Valle Dell'Eden. Semestrale Di Cinema e Audiovisivi* 31:65–82.

Werning, Stefan. 2018b. "Modding as a Strategy to (De)Legitimize Representations of Religion in the Civilization Franchise." In *Discourses of (De)Legitimization: Participatory Culture in Digital Contexts*, edited by Andrew S. Ross and Damian J. Rivers, 307–325. New York: Routledge.

Werning, Stefan. 2019. "Disrupting Video Game Distribution: A Diachronic Affordance Analysis of Steam's Platformization Strategy." *Nordic Journal of Media Studies* 1 (1): 103–124.

White, Hayden. 2014. *Metahistory: The Historical Imagination in Nineteenth-Century Europe*. Baltimore, MD: Johns Hopkins University Press.

Whitson, Jennifer R. 2018. "Voodoo Software and Boundary Objects in Game Development: How Developers Collaborate and Conflict with Game Engines and Art Tools." *New Media and Society* 20 (7): 2315–2332.

Wyss, Beat. 2009. "Das Diapositiv: Oder: Das Ende Der Evidenz." In *PowerPoint: Macht Und Einfluss Eines Präsentationsprogramms*, edited by Wolfgang Coy and Claus Pias, 252–257. Frankfurt: Fischer Taschenbuch Verlag.

Index